SNAPREVISE

SnapRevise Text Guide:
Animal Farm
by George Orwell

Alec Pham

InStudent Education UK Ltd owner of SnapRevise® trademark.
43 Priston Close, Worle, BS22 7FL, Weston-Super-Mare, United Kingdom

www.snaprevise.co.uk

Title: Animal Farm by George Orwell Text Guide
ISBN: 978-1-917424-14-1

Published by InStudent Education UK Ltd CN 15550989 under licence from InStudent Publishing Pty Ltd.
ACN 624 188101

Disclaimer

Preface

Hi all! My name is Alec and like many students, I found English to be a very challenging subject, but with lots of practice, I definitely think that English can become more manageable, and even enjoyable!

Studying English should focus on forming a holistic appreciation of the **content** (i.e. the language, form and structure) and **context** of a piece and subsequently how it is able to construct the world that the composer is attempting to portray. Analysis becomes more important than simply explaining what a certain technique shows. Rather, you should provide a perspective of what it means and how it aligns with the author's purpose in writing the text.

Once you get over this hurdle, it now becomes a matter of answering the essay question in a way that shows the marker you have a thorough understanding of the text. This is something that requires lots of practice, and continual feedback from your peers and teachers.

George Orwell's *Animal Farm* is a great example of why grasping context is essential. Without understanding Orwell's purpose, the novella doesn't hold as much meaning. When studying the text, these are some of many questions to consider: Which individuals do the animals each represent? What was the political and social landscape in 1917? In what ways is the novella relevant to contemporary society? Answering these questions throughout your study should give you a greater knowledge of Orwell's authorial intent.

— Alec Pham

Contents

Section 1

Nutshell Summary

Animal Farm captures the events of the 1917 Russian Revolution. In February 1917, the oppressive and autocratic Tsarist government was overthrown and replaced with the unpopular Provisional Government, which later, in October, was also overthrown, this time by the communist **Bolshevik Party** The aftermath of this rebellion is reincarnated in the form of a **fable**, the events of which reflect the hostile political landscape of Orwell's context and ensuing social injustice.

George Orwell's *Animal Farm* begins in Manor farm, where it is revealed that the drunken farmer Mr Jones has been continually mistreating his animals. Old Major, a wise and esteemed boar now approaching his final days, calls together a meeting, where he tells the other animals of his dream – a **utopian** society, where the farm animals are free to live a life without the burden of slavery by mankind. In this speech, Major declares rebellion to be the key in achieving this idealistic society and patriotically accentuates his speech with the anthem "Beasts of England," which becomes a symbol of the animals' freedom and integrity. Shortly after, Major dies, leaving his dream behind for the other farm animals to achieve.

Plans of rebellion are made, with the pigs establishing themselves as leaders of the coup. With a united effort, the animals are able to drive Mr Jones away from the farm and soon find themselves revelling in freedom. Without the control of Mr Jones, the farm flourishes and the animals experience freedom for the first time in a long time. However, the future of the farm shortly becomes a point of conflict between the established leaders, Snowball and Napoleon, as the two pigs have differing aspirations for the farm. The struggle for power culminates in Snowball eventually being driven away, giving Napoleon total unopposed control over the farm. With Napoleon at the helm, the ideals of equality on the farm seem to quickly vanish, with the pigs slowly establishing control through false claims of **altruism**. Through rhetoric and propaganda, the other animals are compelled to follow the pigs' leadership.

Life on the farm for all the other animals except the pigs becomes inevitably worse under the rule of Napoleon. The rewards of labour on the farm are used to ensure a luxurious lifestyle for the pigs, subsequently subverting the concept of an equal society once proposed by Major. In fact, life on the farm seems to be worse than it had been under the control of Mr Jones. This is symbolically exemplified in the conclusion of the novella, where the other farm animals witness the transformation of the pigs as they begin to walk on two legs and play cards, eerily resembling the humans who oppressed the animals in the first place.

Bolshevik Party: the majority faction of the Russian Social Democratic Party, which seized power in the October Revolution of 1917.

Fable: a short story conveying a moral lesson.

Utopia: a perfect society.

Altruism: selfless concern for the wellbeing of others.

Section 2

Background Information

Eric Arthur Blair (otherwise known by his pen name, George Orwell) was born in 1903 to British colonists within India. He was born into a historically well-established middle-class family that had profited from slavery. Throughout his life, Orwell became a firm believer in **democratic socialism.** This stemmed from a series of life experiences which played a large role in shaping the political undertones within *Animal Farm.*

As a child, Orwell attended St Cyprians School on a scholarship, which he described as being an "expensive and snobbish school." Published **posthumously**, Orwell's essay *Such, Such were the Joys* provided a harrowing perspective of his schooling life and his experiences of mistreatment by the older students, described as "a continuous triumph of strong over the weak." In this sense, Orwell was exposed to an environment of oppression from a young age and was therefore intensely familiar with the hierarchy of power long before he published *Animal Farm.*

Upon graduating college, Orwell opted to serve in the Imperial Police Force in Burma for five years (1922–1927). It was here that he witnessed the pervasive influence of **imperialism** in Burma, where he found himself a part of the group that oppressed and exploited the people. On the side, Orwell spent much of his time away from his peers, instead finding leisure in reading and learning about the culture of Burma. His empathy for the people and resentment towards the classism in Burma was captured in his essay *Shooting an Elephant* and his later published book *Burmese Days*. It can be said that this experience prompted his later guilt over England's complicity in colonialism.

After his time in Burma, Orwell returned to England with the aim of becoming a writer. Inspired by author Jack London's book *The People of the Abyss,* Orwell spent his time exploring the East End of London, an area renowned for its poverty. He would spend the next five years making regular expeditions through the East End, familiarising himself with the lower classes in London. Orwell used these experiences as inspiration for his essays and his first book, *Down and Out in Paris and London* (1933). In 1928, Orwell moved to Paris and became a relatively successful journalist and author, writing many pieces which centred upon the idea of poverty in London. However, his fortunes quickly changed the following year, when he became seriously ill and had his savings stolen, all in the same year (poor guy). As a result, Orwell had to resort to lower-class jobs, which gave him a further insight into the socioeconomic disadvantage experienced by London's working class.

Democratic socialism: a system in which production and wealth are collectively owned but operated under a democracy as opposed to an authoritarian government.

Posthumously: occurring after one's death.

Imperialism: when a country seeks power and influence abroad over other nations, often through exercising military and economic control.

After spending two years in Paris, Orwell returned to London as a writer for *Adelphi,* and as a private tutor. Yet, Orwell seemed to live a sort of double-life, posing as a lower class citizen in an attempt to holistically appreciate the experience of living as one. Despite being part of the middle class, it was obvious that Orwell had a unique interest in the lives of the less fortunate. In 1932, Orwell eventually became a teacher, and it was at this time that a radical and socialist publishing house offered to print one of his books. Afterwards, Orwell would spend his time writing more books, such as *Down and Out in Paris and London.* In these books, Orwell opted to create the pen name "George Orwell" as a way to dissociate his family name from his experiences as a tramp.

In 1936, Orwell was encouraged to spend some time investigating the notoriously poor area of Northern England. Here, he observed the housing conditions, viewed public health records and regularly visited the mines to gain a better understanding of the widespread poverty. Eventually, his time in Northern England culminated in his publication of *Road to Wigan Pier.* The book also included a long essay explaining his support for socialism yet rejected its viability due to the "priggish and dull" figureheads of the movement, and the **proletarian** followers who remained uneducated in socialist ideology.

Proletarian: a member of the working class.

Shortly after marrying a close friend he had met while working at a bookstore, Orwell almost immediately left England to participate in the Spanish Civil War. Concerned with the uprisings of Spanish dictator Francisco Franco's forces, he opted to fight against the fascists in Spain. In order to fight on the Madrid Front in Barcelona, Orwell was required to join a group of communist allies. Although, Orwell did not think much of communism, that was soon to change after this experience, where he witnessed blatantly false propaganda being spread by the Communist press. This soured his views on communism completely.

In early 1937, Orwell was shot in the throat by a sniper, and was subsequently discharged. At this time, there was much debate between Communist factions in Barcelona, which led to George and his wife being labelled as potential threats to the political goals of the Republic. Ultimately, they were able to escape persecution and returned to England, where Orwell would describe his experiences and distaste towards communism in *Homage to Catalonia.*

Later in his life, George was employed by the BBC, broadcasting counter-propaganda to that put forth by Nazi Germany. He soon left his job to focus on writing *Animal Farm*, which was inspired by his time in Spain to a large extent. It was there that he realised "how easily totalitarian propaganda can control the opinion of enlightened people in democratic countries." In this way, he viewed Stalin as being a corrupt figure who distorted the ideals of socialism, and this ultimately prompted him to write *Animal Farm.*

Section 3

Chapter-by-Chapter Analysis

> **KEY POINT :**
> I have organised this chapter-by-chapter analysis according to key quotes, arranged in chronological order, and analysed to reveal what they mean and how they drive the plot forward. This, coupled with the Quote Bank starting on page 45, will provide you with an array of quotes to include and analyse in your responses!

Chapter 1

Banality: commonplace or lacking in originality; obvious and boring.

"Mr Jones, of Manor Farm, had locked the hen-houses for the night, but was too drunk to remember to shut the popholes." Beyond establishing the setting of the novella, the **opening sentence** portrays Mr Jones as a drunken and negligent farm owner, immediately prompting audiences to question the ethical integrity of his character. The matter-of-fact tone establishes a **banality** that suggests that this event is in fact an everyday occurrence.

Autocratic: a ruler with absolute power.

"As soon as the light in the bedroom went out, there was a stirring and fluttering" – the stark **contrast** between Mr Jones' dormancy and the animals' sudden activity reveals a sense of uneasiness amongst the animals of Manor Farm. It suggests that the animals are unwilling to go about their normal routines with Mr Jones in proximity, especially in his drunken state. Through the **characterisation** of Mr Jones as a domineering figure, Orwell generates a contextual understanding of the Tsarist Empire which subjugated the Russian populace through its **autocratic** rule.

Heterodigetic: a heterodigetic narrator is one who does not take part in the plot of the story. (This is particularly common in fables.)

"Old Major (so he was always called, though the name under which he had been exhibited was Willingdon Beauty)." The use of **parentheses** helps to deliberately establish a **heterodiegetic narrative voice** that contextualises the novella as a fable. In this sense, Orwell constructs a political critique that becomes more accessible to a diverse range of audiences due to its **allegorical** form.

Allegory: an extended metaphor in literature used to deliver a message about a wider issue.

"Major was already ensconced on his bed of straw, under a lantern which hung from a beam." This representation of Major combines the historical personalities of Karl Marx and Vladimir Lenin, both of whom were influential forces leading up to the upheaval of the Tsarist regime. Marx was a German philosopher whose political ideas formed the foundations of communism and socialism. Devoted to the ideals of communism, Lenin was a figurehead of the Bolshevik Party and was instrumental in leading the Russian Revolution of 1917. Here, the **visual imagery** is able to subtly capture Major's aura of prominence and defines his status as a revered member of the farm.

"Boxer was an enormous beast, nearly 18 hands high, and as strong as two ordinary horses put together." In this short biographical passage, we are introduced to the other farm animals such as Boxer, who is exemplified as a **stoic** figure through Orwell's **simile**. Boxer is a character of notable importance throughout the chapters of the novella as he **symbolises** the **proletariat**, who endured long and gruelling working hours in poor conditions during the early 20th century.

Stoic: a person who can endure pain or hardship without showing their feelings or complaining.

"What is the nature of this life of ours? Let's face it: our lives are miserable." Major's **hypophora** emphasises the undeniable oppression the animals are faced with under the control of Mr Jones. The **truncated answer** with the use of the **collective pronoun** "our" becomes a bleak summation of life for all on Manor Farm, similarly, capturing the social landscape under the **despotic** autocracy of Tsar Nicholas II. Due to the incompetence of Tsar Nicholas II and Russia's hefty losses in World War I, there was an increasing sense of discontent amongst the population as many people began to question the capabilities of their leader.

Hypophora: a question immediately followed by an answer.

Truncated: shortened or cut-off.

"Those who are capable of it are forced to work to the last atom of our strength." Here, Orwell **hyperbolically** conveys the atmosphere of overarching subjugation on the farm by emphasising the arduous workload that is unfairly placed upon the animals. Here, audiences are provided with insight into the blatant perversion of freedom experienced by the working class.

Despot: a malicious ruler with absolute power.

"The life of an animal is misery and slavery." In this terse sentence, Major **metaphorically** relegates the life of an animal to a simple tool used to benefit mankind and punctuates an inevitable fate that the animals are faced with. Thus, Orwell generates a macabre image of existence that reflected the plight of many citizens in the Russian working class.

Hyperbolic: exaggerated.

Cumulative: the total amount of something when it is all added together.

"This single farm of ours would support a dozen horses, twenty cows, hundreds of sheep." Through **cumulative listing,** Major emphasises the potential of the farm to flourish outside the control of Mr Jones by creating a vision of shared prosperity. His idealistic perspective parallels the concept of communism which called for wealth to be evenly distributed amongst the citizens.

Kairos: a rhetorical concept that involves presenting an argument at the perfect time.

"Why then do we continue in this miserable condition?" Major **rhetorically** coaxes the idea of rebellion by questioning the animals' passivity despite their poor quality of life. Here, he uses **kairos** to encourage the animals to adopt an idiosyncratic mindset and consider the gross injustices of their current system.

"[Man] does not give milk, he does not lay eggs, he is too weak to pull the plough, he cannot run fast enough to catch rabbits." Through **anaphora**, the speech begins to crescendo as Major proceeds to condemn mankind for the continuous struggle that the animals have endured. This particular section of Major's speech emerges as a compelling critique of the Tsarist regime for not contributing in any meaningful way to the plight of the working class.

Anaphora: the use of a word referring back to a word used earlier in a text.

This evokes a sense of empathy that prompts responders to support the animals' rebellion against the humans. Subsequently, audiences are able to appreciate the **power of rhetoric,** which will become a prominent thematic concern throughout the novella.

Bourgeoisie: the middle class who own most of society's wealth and means of production.

"That is my message to you, comrades: Rebellion." The **capitalisation** of Rebellion illustrates its importance as a conclusive goal rather than a simple concept. The idea of rebellion is similarly encapsulated within *the Communist Manifesto*, a political text written by Karl Marx and Friedrich Engels in 1848. Of particular interest is the pamphlet's spiel on **class struggle** – it theorises that the exploitation of the proletariat by the **bourgeoisie** will inevitably lead to social revolution and an overthrow of the capitalist system. This **theory of Permanent Revolution** alone **foreshadows** events that occur later in the story.

Theory of Permanent Revolution: a Marxist theory that stated Russia could only achieve communism through a sustained revolution abroad and domestically.

"And above all, pass on this message of mine to those that come after you, so that future generations shall carry on the struggle until it is victorious." This declaration of unrelenting desire for change is **symbolic** of enlightenment and defection from the old system of rulership. It suggests that change is a gradual process that will require dedication from not only the instigators, but those of future generations.

"All men are enemies. All animals are comrades." – Major's **aphoristic** claim creates a clear division between good and bad, essentially establishing the platform for revolution. It is a vague yet simple concept for the less intelligent animals to understand and unifies the animals against the common threat of human "enemies."

Foreshadow: a warning or indication of a future event.

Aphoristic: a general statement of wisdom of truth.

"As he had said, his voice was hoarse, but he sang well enough, and it was a stirring tune, something between *Clementine* and *La Cuaracha*." The anthem "Beasts of England" becomes intensely **symbolic** of the optimistic desire for change. Its undertones of rebellion ("for freedom's sake") align with the intentions of La Cuaracha, a Spanish folk song dedicated to the Mexican Revolution.

"The birds jumped onto their perches, the animals settled down in the straw, and the whole farm was asleep in a moment." The **tone** of urgency created by the animals in returning to their quiet obedience is a bizarre **contrast** to their previous state of euphoria. Despite Major's speech declaring rebellion, the audience is reminded that the animals are still currently powerless against Jones. This conclusion to the chapter is reminiscent of the events of Bloody Sunday 1905, where citizens who pushed for systemic political and social change were massacred at the hands of the Tsar's Imperial Guard.

Chapter 2

"Three nights later old Major died peacefully in his sleep." The chapter immediately commences with a short homage to Old Major who dies shortly after his declaration of Rebellion. Orwell **historically alludes** to Karl Marx's death in which he was unable to see his own political ideals come to fruition.

"They did not know when the Rebellion predicted by Major would take place, they had no reason for thinking it would be within their own lifetime, but they saw clearly that it was their duty to prepare for it." The **elongated sentence** illustrates the unpredictability of the future for the animals after listening to Major's powerful speech. In conveying this atmosphere of nervous unease, the audience begins to realise the impact that Major has had on the animals – it has completely destabilised their lifestyles to the point where every animal feels the intrinsic responsibility to be prepared for rebellion.

Elongate: to make something longer.

"Organising the others fell naturally upon the pigs, who were generally recognised as being the cleverest of the animals." Already, we can see that the platform for change is **ironically** being utilised as a pedestal for some animals to assert their dominance. In an obvious subversion of Major's declaration that "all animals are equal," the pigs are given a leadership role for the **coup** against Jones due to their intellectual qualities. As such, Orwell expresses the inherent tendencies of human nature to pursue power, thus elucidating his ideals as a democratic socialist rather than a communist.

Coup: a sudden, violent, and illegal seizure of power.

"Napoleon was a large, rather fierce looking Berkshire boar... not much of a talker, but with a reputation of getting his own way." The **characterisation** of Napoleon as a resolute figure parallels the qualities of historical figure **Joseph Stalin**, who notoriously consolidated his power through brutal means during his terroristic reign. "Snowball was a much more vivacious pig than Napoleon, quicker in speech and more inventive" – Snowball's personal traits reflect those of **Leon Trotsky,** who was historically known to be much more eloquent and charismatic. "The others said of Squealer that he could turn black into white" – The **paradoxical** concept of converting black into its directly opposing shade is one that is completely illogical to the reader. Squealer's touted capacity to do so exemplifies his persuasive nature and underpins his ability to manipulate other animals to align with his system of thought.

Paradoxical: seemingly contradictory.

'These three had elaborated Old Major's teachings into a complete system of thought, to which they gave the name of Animalism." The term Animalism emerges as a literary appropriation of communism and encapsulates communist ideals in the sense that it endeavours to delegate equal ownership of land and goods to all animals. One could also say that the word itself draws parallels to the human-equivalent term, **Humanism,** connoting a philosophy that is holistically dedicated to the individualism and value of animals.

Humanism: a philosophy focused on the value of individuals and personal agency.

"They held secret meetings in the barn and expounded the principles of Animalism to the others," suggesting that the passing on of knowledge to the other animals on the farm represents a meaningful desire to rebel against the constraints of their current lives through enlightenment. It illustrates the beginning of a new system of political consciousness, similarly, reflecting the shifting mentality of the Russian populace in the hefty aftermath of WWI.

Enigmatic: difficult to interpret or understand.

"[Moses] claimed to know the existence of a mysterious country called Sugarcandy Mountain." Moses the raven is an **enigmatic** character who does not seem to engage with the plans of rebellion as strongly as the other animals. Rather, he reveals to the other animals the supposed existence of Sugarcandy Mountain, a paradise for those entering the afterlife. Whether this is meant as motivation for the animals or is simply a means of causing controversy remains yet to be seen. However, because he is distastefully known as "Jones' special pet," it is possible that Moses **theological** musings are an attempt to sabotage the work ethic of the farm animals.

Theological: relating to the study of God and religious belief.

"He had become much disheartened after losing money in a lawsuit, and had taken more than was good for him." At face value, this line essentially reveals the reason behind Jones' steady decline from a once "capable farmer" to a negligent alcoholic. But more importantly, it **allegorises** Russia's huge economic losses stemming from their failures at the Eastern Front, leading to dwindling food supplies and a shortage of labour due to **conscription.**

Conscription: compulsory military service.

"His men were idle and dishonest, the field were full of weeds, the buildings wanted roofing, the hedges were neglected, and the animals were underfed." Extending on the previous point, the **accumulation** used in describing the **dilapidated** state of the farm creates an overwhelming image of chaos that encapsulates the profound impacts of WWI. Here, Orwell provides commentary upon the lowly socioeconomic landscape of Russia under the incompetent rulership of Tsar Nicholas II.

Dilapidated: in a state of disrepair or ruin.

"At last they could stand it no longer. One of the cows broke in the door of the store-shed with her horn and all the animals began to help themselves from the bins." After years of oppression by Jones, the animals are pushed to breaking point from starvation, effectively instigating the rebellion in an unexpected way. This reflects the start of the Petrograd riots of February, the first of two revolutions constituting the 1917 Russian Revolution.

"The bits, the nose-rings, the dogchains, the cruel knives with which Mr. Jones had been used to castrate the pigs and lambs, were all flung down the well." The permanent removal of these items of physical repression **metaphorically** illustrates the newfound sense of freedom that the animals have gained. This dramatic image encapsulates the animals' desire to survive within a hostile landscape, foregrounding the inherent human need to rebel against injustice.

"Yes, it was theirs – everything that they could see was theirs!" Coupled with the **repetition** of "was theirs," the exclamation expresses a deep sense of disbelief towards what has been achieved. We can see that the upheaval of the dictatorial system has now evolved into a **bastion** of hope for the animals to pursue a better life.

"[Mollie] had taken a piece of blue ribbon from Mrs. Jones' dressing-table and was holding it against her shoulder and admiring herself in the glass in a very foolish manner." Despite the achievements of the revolution, Mollie seems to be largely unaffected, instead opting to embellish herself with items of **materialistic** beauty. This **character development** helps audiences to understand Mollie as a character who's **hedonistic** desires are prioritised over the wellbeing of her fellow animals, reflecting the conceited values of the upper class during the Russian Revolution.

"The pigs now revealed that during the past three months they had taught themselves to read and write from an old spelling book which had belonged to Mr. Jones' children." The undercurrents of **irony** are becoming increasingly evident to responders – the pigs are using artefacts of human knowledge to further their own education despite their supposedly resolute attitude towards keeping away from human inventions. This act of secrecy not only demonstrates the mental superiority of the pigs, but also reveals a **concomitant** tendency for the pigs to harbour their own private lives.

"These Seven Commandments would now be inscribed on the wall; they would form an unalterable law by which all the animals on Animal Farm must live for ever after." The **religious connotations** of the Seven Commandments serve as a **satirical** mimicry of the Ten Commandments. In doing so, Orwell promotes **communism as an unrealistic philosophy** (a view shaped by his experiences in Spain), that is based upon the idea that all humans are moral, decent and wish for the same ideals. But, as we have already seen through the character of Mollie, this is not necessarily true for all animals, and especially not the pigs.

"So the animals trooped down to the hayfield to begin the harvest, and when they came back in the evening it was noticed that the milk had disappeared." Through the use of **dramatic irony**, the inherent flaws of the Animalist system have already begun to manifest in the closing sentences of the chapter, with the pigs presumably taking the milk for themselves rather than rationing it amongst the other animals.

Bastion: something that strongly and steadfastly maintains principles or attitudes.

Materialistic: excessively concerned with physical possessions and appearances.

Hedonistic: pursuing pleasures.

Concomitant: naturally accompanying or associated.

Chapter 3

"How they toiled and sweated to get the hay in! But their efforts were rewarded, for the harvest was an even bigger success than they had hoped." In stark contrast to their previous labour, we can see that the animals now have a common goal of working towards a better future. "All through that summer the work of the farm went like clockwork" – The connotations of operating machinery in Orwell's **simile** serves to establish this cyclical lifestyle as the new way of life. The farm seems to run autonomously and without fault, prompting responders to initially believe in the integrity of Major's system.

"His answer to every problem, every setback, was 'I will work harder!'" The **simplistic dialogue** of Boxer serves to further **characterise** his nature as a persistent and unquestioning horse who willingly bears the burden of labour for the farm.

"When asked whether he was not happier now that Jones was gone, he would say only 'Donkeys live a long time. None of you has ever seen a dead donkey.'" The intentionally ambiguous **tone** of Benjamin's remark creates a sense of unease for the audiences. It hints at the fact that Benjamin's longevity has allowed him to witness similar events which have ultimately made him wiser and less emotionally invested in the success of the Rebellion compared to the other animals.

"Snowball had found in the harness-room an old green tablecloth of Mrs. Jones' and had painted on it a **hoof and a horn** in white." The green flag of Animal Farm is **symbolic** of the emblem representing the Soviet Union, definitively marking the farm's transition into a socialist state. The hoof and horns are meant to resemble the hammer and sickle.

"It was always the pigs who put forward the resolutions. The other animals understood how to vote but could never think of any resolutions of their own." Orwell again illustrates the obvious intellectual disparity between the pigs and the animals, revealing a growing rift in power between the two parties. We

Oligarchy: a very small group of people having control over a country or organisation.

can see a subtle shift from a democratic society to an **oligarchic** society, as the pigs become the governing power for the farm.

"But it was noticed that these two were never in agreement." Here, we are given insight into the polarising personalities of Snowball and Napoleon. There is an obvious struggle for power between these two, as Orwell **allegorises** the historic struggle between Stalin and Trotsky in their endeavours for political pre-eminence.

"He formed the Egg Production Committee for the hens, the Clean Tails League for the cows, the Wild Comrades' Re-education Committee (the object of this was to tame the rats and rabbits), the Whiter Wool Movement for the sheep, and various others" – the list of Snowball's committees is somewhat **humorous** upon first glance – yet, it exemplifies the prowess of Snowball by illustrating his capacity to create groups tailored for each animal. "The birds did not understand Snowball's long words, but they accepted his explanation," which elucidates the vulnerability of the animals and their inability to discern the language behind Snowball's speech. As such, the gullibility of the animals in their unquestioning acceptance of Snowball's rhetoric serves as a focal point of Orwell's criticism towards the proletariat and their blind trust in their despotic leaders.

"Napoleon took them away from their mothers, saying that he would make himself responsible for their education." The **dramatic irony** of this line generates an atmosphere of unease as audiences are prompted to consider the ulterior motives of Napoleon. It draws a strong parallel with the Hitler Youth, a program designed to indoctrinate the younger generations of Germany with the Nazi ideologies of Adolf Hitler.

"You do not imagine, I hope, that we pigs are doing this in a spirit of selfishness and privilege?" Adhering to the ideals of political propaganda, Squealer utilises the guise of selflessness and altruism to justify the actions of the pigs in taking the apples for themselves. He immediately discredits the preconceived ideas of the animals through the **tone** of disbelief in his **rhetorical question**, in a way that almost blames the animals for being unfairly accusative. "Surely there is no one among you who wants to see Jones come back?" – In Squealer's **rhetorical question**, Jones' abuse of power is **ironically** used as leverage to stifle the qualms of the animals. Squealer commonly uses the practice of fear-mongering to compel the animals to accept the extra privileges that the pigs have acquired.

Chapter 4

"By the late summer the news of what had happened on Animal Farm had spread across half the county." The pervasive influence of the Animal Rebellion across the county reflects the growing belief within rebellion and the opportunity for a new way of life for animals outside of Animal Farm.

"It was lucky that the owners of the two farms which adjoined Animal Farm were on permanently bad terms." The "bad terms" between the farms Foxwood and Pinchfield are used to **allegorically** contextualise the political tensions existing between Great Britain (Mr. Pilkington) and Germany (Mr. Frederick) in the aftermath of World War I.

"Its owner was a Mr. Frederick, a tough, shrewd man, perpetually involved in lawsuits and with a name for driving hard bargains." In stark **contrast** to Mr. Pilkington, who enjoys "fishing or hunting," Mr. Frederick's involvement in lawsuits and bargains fittingly reflects the political and economic predicaments of Germany in the post-WWI era. In particular, the lawsuits represented the demands imposed upon Germany by the **Treaty of Versailles,** which destabilised the country's economic stability and deprived it of its military resources.

Treaty of Versailles: a treaty Germany was forced to sign at the end of WWI, mandating they accept blame for the war and pay back reparations or damages to other nations.

"It was given out that the animals there practised cannibalism, tortured one another with red-hot horseshoes, and had their females in common." The barbaric **imagery** portraying the animals as primitive anarchists underscores a growing fear towards the farm, to the point where the farmers feel the need to slander the animals for the sake of discouraging rebellion within their own estates. These fabrications reflect the innate fears of countries such as Great Britain, who felt threatened by the Russian Revolution, as their status as a world power was weakened by the ensuing events of WWI.

Asyndeton: the omission of conjunctions like 'and' in a list of words or phrases.

"Bulls which had always been tractable suddenly turned savage, sheep broke down hedges and devoured the clover, cows kicked the pail over, hunters refused their fences and shot their riders on to the other side." The **asyndeton** describing the aggressive actions of the animals creates a jumble of clauses that accentuates the tumultuous nature of the animals' rebellion against their owners.

"They were all carrying sticks, except Jones, who was marching ahead with a gun in his hands. Obviously, they were going to attempt the recapture of the farm. This had long been expected, and all preparations had been made. Snowball, who had studied an old book of Julius Caesar's campaigns which he had found in the farmhouse, was in charge of the defensive operations." The return of Jones and his companions echoes the uprising of the White Army, an **amalgamation** of anti-bolshevik parties that endeavoured to restore autocratic rulership in Russia. Here, we also see the strategical **dexterity** skill in performing tasks. of Snowball, reflecting Trotsky in his management of the Bolshevik Red Army in the lead-up to the Russian Civil War.

Amalgamation: combination or collection of things.

Dexterity: skill in performing tasks.

"'I have no wish to take life, not even human life,' repeated Boxer, and his eyes were full of tears." After being inevitably dragged into the feud, the **emotive dialogue** of Boxer conveys the brutalising effect of war upon himself as well as those involved. This mirrors the vast proportion of Red Army soldiers who were inexperienced men conscripted from the proletariat. As such, many were profoundly affected by the outcome of the civil war. This line essentially emerges as a compelling critique of war itself and illustrates how the **sanctity** of human life has become obsolete in the wake of conflict.

Sanctity: ultimate importance and involability.

"War is war. The only good human being is a dead one." The **terse sentence** of Snowball reveals a horrifying reality of war. It reflects the terrifying events of the Red Terror, whereby they used propaganda to justify the slaughter of anti-Bolshevik individuals.

"She had taken to flight as soon as the gun went off." As we have previously seen from her narcissistic personality, Mollie does not wish to partake in any part of the conflict, instead opting to save herself. Her unwillingness to join the rebellion is a focal point of **characterisation** for the upper **echelons** of the Russian society, whose wealth was primarily founded upon the oppression of the working class.

Echelon: a level or rank.

"The animals decided unanimously to create a military decoration, 'Animal Hero, First Class,' which was conferred there and then on Snowball and Boxer... There was also 'Animal Hero, Second Class,' which was conferred posthumously on the dead sheep." Contrary to the Commandment that "all animals are equal," the tiers of military awards **ironically** relegates the sheep to a lower class of heroism despite their deaths in battle. It places emphasis on the idea that sheep are already considered lesser valued members of society, foregrounding the inherent flaws of this supposedly egalitarian society.

"Once on October the twelfth, the anniversary of the Battle of the Cowshed, and once on Midsummer Day, the anniversary of the Rebellion." These battles emerge as literary appropriations of two historical moments leading up to the formation of the Soviet Union – the Russian Civil War and the Russian Revolution of 1917, respectively.

Chapter 5

"She was late for work every morning and excused herself by saying that she had overslept, and she complained of mysterious pains, although her appetite was excellent." The equal workloads distributed to the animals on the farm doesn't sit well with Mollie. We can see that she is one of the few animals who have been disadvantaged or unchanged by the rebellion. Her excuses reveal an unwillingness to adhere to a new lifestyle where she is unable in indulge in lavish human items such as sugar and ribbons.

Without saying anything to the others, [Clover] went to Mollie's stall and turned over the straw with her hoof. Hidden under the straw was a little pile of lump sugar and several bunches of ribbon of different colours." The secret hoard of sugar and ribbons illustrates Mollie's desire to retain her treasures in spite of the new ideals of equality on the farm. This overtly reveals her character as one who is disconnected from the other animals due to her hedonistic personality.

White émigrés: a group of people formed from those who fled Russia in the wake of the Russian Revolution and Russian Civil War. They formed large groups throughout Europe, and many shared the common disliking towards the changed political climate of Russia.

Maxim: a short, pithy statement expressing a general truth or idea.

"Three days later Mollie disappeared. For some weeks nothing was known of her whereabouts." The disappearance of Mollie from the farm historically describes the escape of the aristocrats from Russia following the political transition of the country from an imperialist empire to the era of Bolshevism. As they were faced with the imminent option of either death or exile, many of the Russian nobility sought refuge in other European countries, becoming a part of the group known as the **white émigrés.**

"It was noticed that they were especially liable to break into 'Four legs good, two legs bad' at crucial moments in Snowball's speeches." Orwell plays on the **stereotypical traits** of sheep by depicting them as being mindless followers of Napoleon. Their herd mentality becomes rather problematic for the farm, as their exclamations drown out any chance of rational discussion. This serves to provide social commentary on the way citizens blindly placed their trust in despotic leaders such as Stalin and Hitler. Orwell further critiques the sheep's stupidity because of their **maxim**, "Four legs good, two legs bad," which inaccurately reduces complex political ideals into a simple thought.

"He talked learnedly about field drains, silage, and basic slag, and had worked out a complicated scheme for all the animals to drop their dung directly in the fields." Here, readers learn about the pragmatic approach of Snowball and are given insight into his ideals as a leader. As an intellectual, Snowball seems to advocate the progression of society through the input of the working class.

"After surveying the ground, Snowball declared that this was just the place for a windmill, which could be made to operate a dynamo and supply the farm with electrical power." The development of the windmill on the farm is proposed as a means to reduce the burden of labour on the other animals. It **symbolises** the conceptualisation of Russia's Five-Year Plans, which sought to strengthen Russia's economy through industrialisation.

"Then suddenly he lifted his leg, urinated over the plans, and walked out without uttering a word." Napoleon's contemptuous reaction to Snowball's plans further illustrates the arising tensions between the two, and emerges as an historically accurate depiction of Stalin's perspective towards Trotsky's ideas. Stalin vehemently opposed Trotsky at the time, believing that the current economic policies provided sufficient economic development for the country.

Logical fallacy: use of invalid or flawed reasoning in an argument.

"Napoleon, on the other hand, argued that the great need of the moment was to increase food production, and that if they wasted time on the windmill they would all starve to death." In a similar fashion to Stalin, Napoleon's virtues are **characterised** primarily through his self-centred approach to managing the farm and achieving survival by any means necessary. Napoleon's opposition to the windmill is grounded in a **logical fallacy,** as he essentially asserts that the only way to survive would be to listen to him.

"Windmill or no windmill, he said, life would go on as it had always gone on – that is, badly." The **terse description** of the future as going "badly" by Benjamin serves to **foreshadow** the inevitability of the fate that the animals are confronted with, irrespective of whether Snowball or Napoleon is in charge. Audiences do not understand the rationale behind Benjamin's prediction, yet its enigmatic nature undeniably prompts them to consider the possibility of his comment.

"At this there was a terrible baying sound outside, and nine enormous dogs wearing brass-studded collars came bounding into the barn." The sudden introduction of the dogs sparks an epiphany for the audience as they begin to understand Napoleon's intentions behind his desire to take care of the dogs. His use for the dogs as his personal security force echoes the NKVD, the secret police force that Stalin used to purge those who were opposed to his regime.

"Snowball was racing across the long pasture that led to the road. He was running as only a pig can run, but the dogs were close on his heels." Snowball's escape from the farm marks the start of an unopposed reign for Napoleon. It parallels the exile of Leon Trotsky from Russia following his removal from the **Politburo** and ultimately, the Soviet Union. Despite his exile, Trotsky was still the target of several assassination attempts over the years, even within the comfort of his own home.

Politburo: a small group responsible for the creation of policies within a communist party.

"It was noticed that they wagged their tails to him in the same way as the other dogs had been used to do to Mr. Jones." The inclusion of this minute detail creates an ominous comparison between Napoleon and Mr. Jones. It prompts readers to appreciate the Napoleon's subtle transition into a villainous dictator, much like Mr. Jones was.

"He announced that from now on the Sunday-morning Meetings would come to an end. They were unnecessary, he said, and wasted time." The dissolution of Sunday morning Meetings **symbolises** a loss of unity and democracy amongst the farm, as it means that the animals are no longer able to gather to discuss matters.

"But suddenly the dogs sitting round Napoleon let out deep, menacing growls, and the pigs fell silent and sat down again." The immediate reaction of the pigs to the dogs illustrates the terroristic repression of the individual amidst a hostile political landscape, to the point where free speech no longer becomes a right.

"'Bravery is not enough,' said Squealer. 'Loyalty and obedience are more important.'" The **dialogue** of Squealer primarily encapsulates the essence of Napoleon's regime. Its success is purely driven by the subjugation of individuals as opposed to patriotic spirit, connoting a political ideology that is more akin to totalitarianism than to democracy.

Disinter: to dig up.

Memento mori: a Latin term meaning 'remember you will die,' used to refer to reminders of mortality and the transience of life.

Collectivisation: an agricultural policy adopted by the Soviet Union which endeavoured to change individual farms into state-controlled land.

Pravda: one of the most influential pro-Communist newspapers following the October Russian Revolution.

"The skull of old Major, now clean of flesh, had been **disinterred** from the orchard and set up on a stump at the foot of the flagstaff, beside the gun." Despite recent events, the **memento mori** of Major's skull serves as a bastion of inspiration for the animals to continue the work that was started by Major. It emerges as a solemn reminder of the sacrifices that must be made to achieve the utopian society that was previously envisioned. Historically, it aligns with the public display of Lenin's embalmed corpse in Red Square.

"Napoleon, with Squealer and another pig named Minimus, who had a remarkable gift for composing songs and poems, sat on the front of the raised platform, with the nine young dogs forming a semicircle round them, and the other pigs sitting behind. The rest of the animals sat facing them in the main body of the barn" – The **visual imagery** of this assembly **metaphorically** illustrates the current hierarchy of the farm, with Napoleon and the pigs at the forefront. The animals are no longer considered to be equals, as Napoleon's raised platform becomes **symbolic** of his overarching power over the rest of the farm and his status as an authoritarian figure.

"Napoleon read out the orders for the week in a gruff soldierly style, and after a single singing of Beasts of England, all the animals dispersed." Along with its **blunt tone**, the **methodical structure** of this sentence portrays a setting that is both banal and gloomy.

"The building of the windmill, with various other improvements, was expected to take two years" – Napoleon's decision to continue with the construction of the windmill **allegorises** Stalin's eventual approval of the first Five Year Plan which endeavoured to build economic power through industrialisation and **collectivisation.**

"The windmill was, in fact, Napoleon's own creation. Why, then, asked somebody, had he spoken so strongly against it? Here Squealer looked very sly. That, he said, was Comrade Napoleon's cunning." Here, we begin to see the reconstruction of history by Squealer as he lies to portray Napoleon as the mastermind behind the plans of the windmill. It becomes strongly reminiscent of Stalin's cult of personality, which sought to epitomise Stalin as an icon of Soviet culture. This positive image was mainly upheld through propaganda, the work of **Pravda** being the most notable.

Chapter 6

"All that year the animals worked like slaves." Orwell's **simile** is **ironic** in the fact that the animals believe that they work like slaves. However, the reality is that the animals *are* slaves, but are too naïve to believe otherwise. Their steadfast belief in the system allows them to be manipulated by the pigs, as we have seen multiple times in the previous chapters.

"Throughout the spring and summer they worked a sixty-hour week, and in August Napoleon announced that there would be work on Sunday afternoons as well." The insurmountable workload of the animals realistically mirrors the standards of labour imposed upon the Russian citizens in order to achieve the Five Year Plan.

"To see him toiling up the slope inch by inch, his breath coming fast, the tips of his hoofs clawing at the ground, and his great sides matted with sweat, filled everyone with admiration." The **visual imagery** of Boxer's resilience and work ethic is used to emphasise the physical toll of labour on the proletariat. It suggests that they are the ones who are most affected by these excessive work shifts.

"If they had no more food than they had had in Jones' day, at least they did not have less." Even though food rations are no better than before, the narrator's **understatement** seems to brush this aside by reasoning that the conditions are no worse than when Jones was still around. It is a rather illogical line of thinking, especially considering that the animals once aspired for the farm to be a utopia.

"From now onwards Animal Farm would engage in trade with the neighbouring farms." Despite declaring humans as enemies, Napoleon hypocritically asserts the need to acquire materials from other farms. His exploitation of the rules as a leader is masqueraded as a desire to assist the progression of Animal Farm, yet it comes at the expense of the animals' own resources.

"The needs of the windmill must override everything else, he said." Napoleon's firm claim essentially emerges as a **metaphor** of his prioritisation of the farm over the individual welfare of its inhabitants. "Had not these been among the earliest resolutions passed at that first triumphant Meeting after Jones was expelled? All the animals remembered passing such resolutions: or at least they thought that they remembered it." The pigs' manipulation of the other animals has subsequently created an ambiguous boundary between truths and lies, as the **rhetorical question** captures their sense of doubt towards their own perceptions of the past. "A Mr. Whymper, a solicitor living in Willingdon, had agreed to act as intermediary between Animal Farm and the outside world" – Mr. Whymper **represents** the first capitalists who agreed to establish a trading relationship with the Soviet Union, despite knowing of Stalin's despotic dictatorship.

"Are you certain that this is not something that you have dreamed, comrades? Have you any record of such a resolution? Is it written down anywhere?" Squealer **repetitively questions** the animals in an attempt to undermine their recollection of past events, asserting written law as the sole source of concrete truth. Here, Orwell metonymises human memory as a written record, illustrating the pervasive influence of the oligarchy upon an individual to the point where individual memory is suppressed.

"And since it was certainly true that nothing of the kind existed in writing, the animals were satisfied that they had been mistaken." Here, readers see that the animals are easily led into believing that their versions of the past are wrong, opting to place their trust in the pigs.

"And yet, against their will, they had developed a certain respect for the efficiency with which the animals were managing their own affairs." Despite the constant state of subjugation that the animals are placed in, the humans acknowledge the productivity of the farm, primarily because the pigs are now adopting the role of the oppressive farmer. It reflects the undeniable success of Stalin's Five-Year Plans, prompting other communist states such as China to implement their own practices of long-term economic planning.

"It was also more suited to the dignity of the Leader (for of late he had taken to speaking of Napoleon under the title of 'Leader') to live in a house than in a mere sty." The **parentheses** by the narrator serves to illustrate the gradual evolution of Napoleon from a "comrade" to a title of prominence. This drastic transition espouses the pigs' abandonment of equality on the farm in their pursuit for total overarching power.

"Yes, there it lay, the fruit of all their struggles, levelled to its foundations." The **tone of finality** in this line highlights the sense of trepidation felt by the animals upon witnessing the remains of the windmill. Its collapse is a devastating plot point for the characters of the story, considering all the hard work that was put into its construction.

"'Do you know the enemy who has come in the night and overthrown our windmill? SNOWBALL'!'" – Rather than take responsibility for planning the poor structural foundations of the windmill, Napoleon instead uses this as an opportunity to smear the reputation of Snowball through his **hypophora**. In a similar fashion to Stalin's defamation of Trotsky, Napoleon portrays Snowball as an antagonist of the farm to compel the other animals to continue to work against a common threat.

"Comrades, here and now I pronounce the death sentence upon Snowball." In a clear **subversion** of Major's ideals, Napoleon urges the other animals to kill their former comrade. Through this expression of brutality, Orwell explores the inevitability of violence in a regime where absolute power is enforced.

"Almost immediately the footprints of a pig were discovered in the grass at a little distance from the knoll. They could only be traced for a few yards, but appeared to lead to a hole in the hedge." The presence of these footprints is a slightly perplexing for audiences – it suggests Snowball's potential role as a saboteur, yet it could also indicate a cunning ploy by Napoleon to frame Snowball. Instead, it is left as a point of ambiguity for responders to interpret.

"Forward, comrades! Long live the windmill! Long live Animal Farm!" This string of **anaphoric exclamations** by Napoleon serves to bolster the morale of the animals by uniting them to work towards the progression of the farm. It is a common rhetoric technique that is used by both Squealer and Napoleon to sway the animals to obey their wishes.

Chapter 7

"It was a bitter winter. The stormy weather was followed by sleet and snow, and then by a hard frost which did not break till well into February." The introduction of a cold and hostile setting uses **pathetic fallacy** to foreground the imminent difficulties that the animals are going to be faced with.

"For days at a time the animals had nothing to eat but chaff and mangels. Starvation seemed to stare them in the face." The **personification** of starvation as a staring presence highlights its widespread influence on the farm. Orwell contextually alludes to the Soviet Famine of 1932, whereby several millions of people perished due to poor harvest. This was further compounded by the increased need for food caused by the ongoing process of industrialisation in Russia.

"However, a few selected animals, mostly sheep, were instructed to remark casually in his hearing that rations had been increased." Here, we are able to see the power of Napoleon in manipulating the exteriority of the farm such that it is perceived as a prospering land by others. By creating this image, Napoleon subsequently preserves his credibility to outsiders and consolidates his power as a ruler.

"Napoleon had accepted, through Whymper, a contract for four hundred eggs a week." Orwell further contextualises the circumstances of Stalin's Five Year Plan, which involved the surrendering of resources by the wealthier peasants (also known as the Kulaks) to distribute to the lower classes of peasants in an attempt to collectivise agriculture.

"Led by three young Black Minorca pullets, the hens made a determined effort to thwart Napoleon's wishes. Their method was to fly up to the rafters and there lay their eggs, which smashed to pieces on the floor." For the first time in Napoleon's reign as leader, audiences witness a minor rebellion by the hens of the farm. In a similar fashion to the **Kulaks** a class of wealthy peasants who privately owned land and livestock. The process of collectivisation had a large economic toll on the Kulaks, and as such they strongly rebelled against the new economic policies proposed by Stalin.who disagreed with the idea of collectivisation, the hens defy the orders of Napoleon, illustrating the growing sense of displeasure amongst the animals.

Kulaks: a class of wealthy peasants who privately .

"For five days the hens held out, then they capitulated and went back to their nesting boxes. Nine hens had died in the meantime." Audiences are provided with insight into the futility of action against an oppressive state through the resultant deaths during the hens' rebellion. "It was well seasoned, and Whymper had advised Napoleon to sell it; both Mr. Pilkington and Mr. Frederick were anxious to buy it. Napoleon was hesitating between the two, unable to make up his mind." Napoleon's options to sell to either Pilkington or Frederick reflects the USSR's ambiguous alliances with both Germany and Great Britain, which would not be revealed until the onset of WWII.

"He stole the corn, he upset the milkpails, he broke the eggs, he trampled the seedbeds, he gnawed the bark off the fruit trees." The sudden and tumultuous reintroduction of Snowball through Orwell's **asyndeton** serves to immediately re-establish Snowball's role as an opponent to Napoleon's leadership. Paralleling Trotsky's vocal denunciation of the Soviet bureaucracy as a refugee outside of Russia, Snowball's vandalism aims to destabilise the rule of Napoleon by creating social unrest.

"They all remembered, or thought they remembered, how they had seen Snowball charging ahead of them at the Battle of the Cowshed." Again, we see the interplay between history and memory through the **doubtful tone** of the animals in recollecting the events of the Battle of Cowshed. The questioning of memory becomes a **motif** in the story that is utilised by Orwell to examine the dramatic manipulation of individual thought within the parameters of an oligarchic society such as the USSR.

"'Ah, that is different!' said Boxer. 'If Comrade Napoleon says it, it must be right.'" The mention of Napoleon's name surprisingly seems to resolve Boxer's initially conflicted outlook. His naïve response, "it must be right" demonstrates the blind trust that he along with the other animals are placing in Napoleon. The passivity and lack of insight by the rest of the animals continues to place them in a position of vulnerability, allowing the pigs to resume their corruption.

"'That is the true spirit, comrade!' cried Squealer, but it was noticed he cast a very ugly look at Boxer with his little twinkling eyes." The deliberate inclusion of this minor yet crucial detail reveals Squealer's enthusiasm to be a part of his duplicitous façade. It is this disguise that compels the animals to continue working under the leadership of Napoleon.

"Napoleon now called upon them to confess their crimes. They were the same four pigs as had protested when Napoleon abolished the Sunday Meetings.' Napoleon now assumes the role of the judge in a courtroom, calling upon animals to be tried for their crimes. Orwell alludes to the widely publicised **Moscow Trials**, which were staged to eliminate high ranking Communist party officials deemed as a threat to Stalin's rulership.

Visceral:
relating to deep, inward feelings rather than thoughts and intellect.

"And so the tale of confessions and executions went on, until there was a pile of corpses lying before Napoleon's feet and the air was heavy with the smell of blood, which had been unknown there since the expulsion of Jones." Orwell's **macabre imagery** of the executions elucidates the horrifying fate for those who dare to act against the dictatorship of Napoleon. This particular scene emerges as a deeply **visceral** rendition of the Great Purge of 1936, in which Stalin ordered the mass murder of thousands of people whom he suspected to be dissenters or threats against the Soviet Union.

"'The solution, as I see it, is to work harder. From now onwards I shall get up a full hour earlier in the mornings.'" Working becomes the sole reason for Boxer to persist despite the recent killings on the farm. It becomes a motto for him to abide by and could even be considered his coping mechanism. Yet, the simplicity of his response to the executions prompts responders to consider how the animals are so blinded to the realities of Napoleon's cruelties that they are unable to confront them at all.

"The grass and the bursting hedges were gilded by the level rays of the sun. Never had the farm – and with a kind of surprise they remembered that it was their own farm, every inch of it their own property – appeared to the animals so desirable a place." The appealing **visual imagery** is a stark **contrast** to what has actually happened on the farm. It illustrates a need for the animals to seek catharsis through a meaningful connection with the landscape, as its superficial beauty becomes a beacon of hope.

"If she herself had had any picture of the future, it had been of a society of animals set free from hunger and the whip, all equal, each working according to his capacity, the strong protecting the weak." Clover's idealised depiction of the future reveals an inherent desire to break away from the terrifying reality she is currently faced with. Subsequently, responders are prompted to empathise with her struggles as an individual.

"But still, it was not for this that she and all the other animals had hoped and toiled. It was not for this that they had built the windmill and faced the bullets of Jones' gun." Orwell's use of **anaphora** serves to accentuate the sacrifices the animals have made to work for a better future, but instead have been presented with the complete opposite. It adds a layer of complexity to her character – we see that Clover, along with the other animals, is not just an oppressed worker. She is an animal that desires freedom and peace, values that resonate strongly within our own contemporary society. Thus, Orwell provides social commentary upon the dehumanising nature of totalitarian regimes by critiquing their valuation of power over individual agency and emotion.

"At last, feeling this to be in some way a substitute for the words she was unable to find, she began to sing Beasts of England. The other animals sitting round her took it up, and they sang it three times over." Despite this dark atmosphere, the animals muster the courage to sing the anthem that was initially responsible for their unity. The song is an emblem of hope for the animals that utopian dream can still be achieved through perseverance.

"He announced that, by a special decree of Comrade Napoleon, Beasts of England had been abolished. From now onwards it was forbidden to sing it." Squealer's announcement of the song's abolition marks the profound loss of a culture centred upon freedom and optimism. The replacement song orchestrated by Minimus ("Animal Farm, Animal Farm, Never through me shalt thou come to harm!") now places a heightened focus on the state rather than the individual, resembling the ruthless society that Napoleon has forged for himself and the pigs.

"But somehow neither the words nor the tune ever seemed to the animals to come up to Beasts of England." The **tone of reminiscence** in the closing lines of the chapter gives insight into the sense of repressed dissatisfaction felt by the other animals. They clearly don't value the new song as much as the song that was the reason for their rebellion.

Chapter 8

"It ran: 'No animal shall kill any other animal without cause.' Somehow or other, the last two words had slipped out of the animals' memory." The alteration of the Seven Commandments becomes a common practice for the pigs to justify their atrocious actions against the ideals of Animalism. As such, Orwell comments upon the manipulative nature of totalitarian regimes, asserting their egotistical tendencies to fulfil their own goals rather than uphold the wellbeing of the citizens.

Epithets: adjective or descriptive phrase to describe a person.

"This pigs liked to invent for him such titles as Father of All Animals, Terror of Mankind, Protector of the Sheep-fold, Ducklings' Friend, and the like." Echoing Stalin's cult of personality, Orwell's **list of glorified epithets** captures the widespread influence of Napoleon across the farm. Through rhetoric and propaganda, Napoleon is now idolised as a perfect leader to the people despite his crimes on the farm. It becomes an ominous reminder of how language and media can completely destabilise the notions of truth within society.

"You would often hear one hen remark to another, 'Under the guidance of our Leader, Comrade Napoleon, I have laid five eggs in six days.'" Napoleon now becomes the sole reason for the successes of the farm, and the other animals unquestioningly adopt this system of thought, as they **paradoxically** assert "Comrade Napoleon" to be their "Leader." We see here that this embellishment of Napoleon becomes a significant part of societal **orthodoxy** of the ordinary or usual type. as a result of Squealer's propaganda.

Orthodoxy: system of ideology.

"Three hens had come forward and confessed that, inspired by Snowball, they had entered into a plot to murder Napoleon." – This revelation of Snowball's ongoing role as an **agent provocateur** conveys the ever-present rebellion that exists against Napoleon's dictatorship. It reflects the numerous assassination attempts that were taken out against Napoleon during his years as ruler.

Agent provocateur: an individual who breaks the law or pushes others to break the law to smear someone's reputation.

"At about the same time it was given out that Napoleon had arranged to sell the pile of timber to Mr. Pilkington." Orwell **allegorises** the initially stable relationship between Russia and the West (the US and UK), with Germany seemingly being the common enemy in the lead-up to WWII.

"He had flogged an old horse to death, he starved his cows, he had killed a dog by throwing it into the furnace, he amused himself in the evenings by making cocks fight with splinters of razor-blade tied to their spurs." The horrific **visual imagery** of torture created by Orwell serves to exemplify the atrocities of Hitler prior to WWII. Frederick's depraved treatment of the animals parallels Hitler's heinous acts against the Jewish population.

"The pigeons who were still sent out to spread **tidings** of the Rebellion were forbidden to set foot anywhere on Foxwood, and were also ordered to drop their former slogan of 'Death to Humanity' in favour of 'Death to Frederick.'" As a primary facet of a totalitarian society, propaganda is used to drive the animals into placing their support behind the political decisions of Napoleon in favouring a potential deal with Pilkington.

"In the teeth of every difficulty, in spite of inexperience, of primitive implements, of bad luck and of Snowball's treachery, the work had been finished punctually to the very day!" The **anaphoric exclamation** conveys a deep sense of achievement towards the completion of the windmill's construction and a sense of hope for the animals, despite the various hardships that the animals have been faced with.

"He personally congratulated the animals on their achievement and announced that the mill would be named Napoleon Mill." Napoleon's **eponymous** naming of the windmill signifies a profound narcissism inherently stemming from his constant abuse of power. This subtle **characterisation** of Napoleon as egocentric becomes a focal point of critique for Orwell, as he condemns totalitarian dictators for their relentless pursuit of power.

"Throughout the whole period of his seeming friendship with Pilkington, Napoleon had really been in secret agreement with Frederick." This sudden change in mindset parallels Russia's decision to backtrack on their initial alliances with the West and sign the **Molotov-Ribbentrop Pact** (also known as the Nazi-Soviet Non-Aggression Pact) with Germany, a major event which influenced Germany's decision to invade Poland at the start of WWII. "The news of what had happened sped round the farm like wildfire. The banknotes were forgeries! Frederick had got the timber for nothing!" – Orwell's **series of exclamations** captures the overarching sense of shock on the farm towards Frederick's betrayal, highlighting the way in which Germany dramatically broke the pact to invade the Soviet Union in Operation Barbarossa on June 22, 1941.

"The animals could not face the terrible explosions and the stinging pellets, and in spite of the efforts of Napoleon and Boxer to rally them, they were soon driven back." The animals' retreat against Frederick conveys their lack of preparation and resources, much like the USSR in the face of Germany's **Blitzkrieg** approach to war. Here, Orwell historically illustrates the Battle of Stalingrad, one of the largest battles in modern warfare in which Russia suffered deep losses to their army.

"One of them bearing a scrap of paper from Pilkington. On it was pencilled the words: 'Serves you right.'" Pilkington's message of retaliation emerges as a **satirical** depiction of the Allies' initial unwillingness to participate in the war, with one reason being due to Russia's decision to side with Germany.

"It was as though the windmill had never been." The **short sentence** serves to create a dramatic effect, positioning audiences to appreciate the profound nature of the animals' loss. It reflects the magnitude of the losses that Russia experienced in the aftermath of the war with Germany, which included over one million soldiers dying on the Stalingrad front.

"He called the animals together and told them that he had a terrible piece of news to impart. Comrade Napoleon was dying!" Orwell's **exclamation** is **humorous**, in that Squealer expresses Napoleon's current state as a cause for concern. However, readers can readily deduce that Napoleon is feeling the effects of a hangover, and that the pigs are new to the experience of binge drinking. Further, we see that the pigs are indulging in habits pertinent to humans, demonstrating the insidious transition of the pigs.

"It was learned that he had instructed Whymper to purchase in Willingdon some booklets on brewing and distilling." Orwell's **dramatic irony** in the pigs wishing to acquire knowledge on brewing and distilling conveys their tendencies for self-indulgence. Yet, it is narrated in a way that seems innocent and unknowing, highlighting the way in which the animals continue to remain ignorant of the truth. "Squealer, temporarily stunned, was sprawling beside it, and near at hand there lay a lantern, a paint-brush, and an overturned pot of white paint." – There is further **dramatic irony** in this scene as we are now given concrete evidence of Squealer's role in the alteration of the Seven Commandments.

"None of the animals could form any idea as to what this meant, except old Benjamin, who nodded his muzzle with a knowing air, and seemed to understand, but would say nothing." Benjamin seems to be the only character who understands what is transpiring on the farm yet is too passive to alert the animals as to what is going on. It is possible that Benjamin is too disinterested with the matters of the farm to tell the animals of the pigs' blatant exploitation. However, another reason could be that he has been witness to this type of corruption before, and feels that his input would have no impact in the end, as he has previously suggested in Chapter 5: "life would go on as it had always gone on – that is, badly."

Denouement:
the final part of a narrative in which the strands of the plot are drawn together and matters are explained or resolved.

"Actually the Commandment read: 'No animal shall drink alcohol to excess.'" Drawing parallels to the start of Chapter 8, we see that once again, the Commandments have been changed to accommodate the needs of the pigs. The use of this observation as the chapter's **denouement** insidiously reveals to audiences the extent of the pigs' moral descent.

Chapter 9

"For a horse, it was said, the pension would be five pounds of corn a day and, in winter, fifteen pounds of hay, with a carrot or possibly an apple on public holidays. Boxer's twelfth birthday was due in the late summer of the following year." Considering the events of the past few chapters, the conversation surrounding Boxer's retirement seems to be the sole source of optimism for the farm. As he is known to be the hardest worker, the potential of a good life after work for Boxer prompts the audience's empathy.

"A too rigid equality in rations, Squealer explained, would have been contrary to the principles of Animalism." The **illogical comment** made by Squealer is a complete contradiction to Major's tenet "all animals are equal". The subversion of this ideal reflects how elite members of the Communist Party were favoured and given a majority of the resources that the proletariat worked for.

"(Squealer always spoke of it as a 'readjustment,' never as a 'reduction')." The narrator's input within the **parentheses** further underscores the manipulative rhetoric of Squealer, as he opts to use more enticing synonyms in phrasing his ideas to the other animals.

"Reading out the figures in a shrill, rapid voice, he proved to them in detail that they had more oats, more hay, more turnips than they had had in Jones' day, that they worked shorter hours, that their drinking water was of better quality, that they lived longer." The **cumulative list** of declarations made by Squealer is used to reinforce the positive social and economic changes which have been elicited as a result of the animals' labour. However, these claims have no logical nor statistical basis to support them, and one can presume this is another one of Squealer's deceitful tactics to provide the animals with motivation to continue working. Thus, Orwell conveys how objective information becomes perverted in propaganda.

"They took their exercise in the garden, and were discouraged from playing with the other young animals." Class **stratification** becomes an inevitable facet of this society, as even the younger generations of animals are separated into their castes.

'Pigs, of whatever degree, were to have the privilege of wearing green ribbons on their tails on Sundays." This line is **ironic**, considering the animals' intense scrutiny of Mollie for her desire to wear a ribbon earlier in the story. Previously condemned as a "badge of slavery" in Chapter 2 by Snowball, the ribbon is now championed as an item of privilege and beauty. Hence, responders can appreciate the transformation of the pigs as they adopt Mollie's propensities for glamour and relinquish their values in exchange for self-indulgence.

Stratification: arrangement or classification of something into different groups.

"Rations, reduced in December, were reduced again in February, and lanterns in the stalls were forbidden to save Oil." The **capitalisation** of Oil places a heightened importance on its role as a valued commodity to the pigs, placing it as a priority over the needs of the other animals.

"But the pigs seemed comfortable enough, and in fact were putting on weight if anything." Orwell's **juxtaposition** between the quality of life for the pigs and the rest of the animals presents a glaring disparity that highlights how the pigs are the sole beneficiaries from this society.

"At the appointed time the animals would leave their work and march round the precincts of the farm in military formation, with the pigs leading, then the horses, then the cows, then the sheep, and then the poultry." In this chapter, Orwell explores the decadent lifestyle that the pigs have acquired through their gradual exploitation of the farm. The spontaneous demonstrations emerge as grandiose displays of their superiority on the farm, as their celebrations are focused upon the idolisation of Napoleon ("Long live Comrade Napoleon!").

"Afterwards there were recitations of poems composed in Napoleon's honour and a speech by Squealer giving particulars of the latest increases in the production of foodstuffs, and on occasion a shot was fired from the gun." The inclusion of poems as a celebratory tribute emphasises how literature has been altered to historically manipulate the societal perception of Napoleon. Further, the gunshot, originally used to mark the anniversaries of significant battles, is now used profusely as an act of celebration, thus underscoring a lack of respect towards the sacrifices the animals have made in war.

"[Moses] was quite unchanged, still did no work, and talked in the same strain as ever about Sugarcandy Mountain." Moses' mysterious re-introduction is rather strange – he seems to not have changed since the Rebellion, and still preaches the same values about Sugarcandy Mountain. It subsequently prompts audience speculation towards the author's intent behind the inclusion of Moses as a character. "Many of the animals believed him. Their lives now, they reasoned, were hungry and laborious; was it not right and just that a better world should exist somewhere else?" – The pessimistic **rhetorical question** lays the foundations for the animals' **nihilistic** sense of displacement within the world. Their collective belief within Moses' claims further highlights their deep-rooted desires for a world where they are not oppressed, much like their aspirations at the start of the novella.

Nihilistic: the rejection of all religious and moral principles in the belief that life is meaningless.

"They all declared contemptuously that his stories about Sugarcandy Mountain were lies, and yet they allowed him to remain on the farm, not working, with an allowance of a gill of beer a day." Here, the pigs' cynical perception of Moses remains the same. Yet, their passivity in allowing Moses to remain on the farm expresses a subtle approval towards his religious discourse. Moses' speeches of paradise seem to subdue the animals to a certain extent, and as such, the pigs are happy for this to continue.

"It was only his appearance that was a little altered; his hide was less shiny than it had used to be, and his great haunches seemed to have shrunken." Through this **imagery**, we see that Boxer, who once presented as the epitome of hope and hard work, has now been significantly impacted by the effects of labour and war.

"'Boxer has fallen! He is lying on his side and can't get up!'" In these exclamations, Orwell punctuates the downfall of Boxer and presents to responders an image of helplessness. It is a confronting reality for many, as audiences come to realise that one of the most resilient characters of the novella no longer has the physical capacity to cope with the burden of work.

"'Fools! Fools!' shouted Benjamin, prancing round them and stamping the earth with his small hoofs. 'Fools! Do you not see what is written on the side of that van?'" Benjamin's **epizeuxis** is a dramatic deviation from his normal character, as he finally speaks to attempt to save Boxer from his imminent death. Within the previous chapters, Boxer is noted to be one of Benjamin's few friends, and so Benjamin's assertion incites empathy, as audiences recognise the care he has for his friend. "Boxer was never seen again" – The **truncated sentence** dramatically presents the finality of Boxer's fate, marking the loss of a character who in many ways withstood hardship and despair.

Epizeuxis: the repetition of a word or phrase in quick succession for emphasis.

"Three days later it was announced that he had died in the hospital at Willingdon, in spite of receiving every attention a horse could have." In spite of this announcement, audiences know that Boxer has most probably been put down, a brutal image that starkly polarises the conditions surrounding Boxer's death that were put forth by the pigs. Furthermore, "the word went round that from somewhere or other the pigs had acquired the money to buy themselves another case of whisky." This crucial detail at the end of the chapter offers audiences a dramatic **epiphany** as Boxer's fate is elucidated – the pigs have exchanged Boxer's life to acquire more money for alcohol. This blatant dismissal of life in the pursuit of personal gain is something that has now pushed the pigs to an unprecedented level of moral depravity, as responders are now confronted with the horrifying realities of a dystopian society.

Chapter 10

"Years passed. The seasons came and went, the short animal lives fled by." The **temporal shift** established at the start of the chapter immediately prompts responders to consider the fate of all the characters on the farm, and whether the animals have been driven to rebellion, or have been relegated further into a state of total subjugation.

Temporal: related to time.

"Only old Benjamin was much the same as ever, except for being a little greyer about the muzzle, and, since Boxer's death, more **morose** and **taciturn** than ever." The deeply despondent personality of Benjamin serves to remind the audiences of his loss, and how it has affected him throughout the years. Napoleon's claim of an ideal lifestyle is deeply **ironic** in the sense that audiences know that he neither works hard nor lives a modest lifestyle. Thus, Orwell points out the hypocrisy of the pigs in imposing this societal orthodoxy, but not adhering to this themselves.

"But still, neither pigs nor dogs produced any food by their own labour; and there were very many of them, and their appetites were always good." Orwell depicts the dogs and pigs as being parasitic in nature, depleting the resources of the farm yet doing nothing to contribute. Their statuses as members of the upper echelons of society become clear, as they are given the benefits of privilege and power.

"As for the others, their life, so far as they knew, was as it had always been. They were generally hungry, they slept on straw, they drank from the pool, they laboured in the field." Here, audiences are able to see the current state of society under the dictatorship of Napoleon. In reducing the animals' daily routines to a simple list of tasks, Orwell's **asyndeton** establishes the banality of life on the farm, demonstrating how nothing has changed for the animals.

"They could not remember. There was nothing with which they could compare their present lives." The continual repression of the animals' memories has subsequently deteriorated their ability to distinguish between reality and imagination. Due to the propagandistic methods of Squealer, memory no longer becomes a reliable source to trace history, and as such, there is no way to holistically draw upon past experiences. "Hunger, hardship, and disappointment being, so he said, the unalterable law of life" – Benjamin's triad **aphoristically** characterises life as being an inevitable cycle of turmoil despite its small moments of glory. He adopts a pre-determinist worldview, asserting that the animals hold no agency over their fate. In considering this, it could thus be suggested that this mindset is the reason why Benjamin has chosen to remain uninvolved in the Rebellion, as he realises that the outcome will always be the same no matter what actions are taken.

"Even the tune of Beasts of England was perhaps hummed secretly here and there." Despite the years of oppression that the animals have faced, the legacy of hope and rebellion remains in the form of the song Beasts of England. It no longer becomes an icon of freedom, but rather it now **symbolises** a secret communal yearning for change. Strangely, this sentiment is one that was similarly present in the opening chapter when Jones was in power, thus delineating the storyline's cyclical process of rebellion and repression.

"It was a pig walking on his hind legs." The **short sentence** isolated in a paragraph encapsulates the animals' sense of shock, as the audiences are presented with an image that is both absurd and disturbing. It emerges as a physical manifestation of their transformation into despotic rulers, with the pigs coming to resemble the humans that oppressed them.

"He carried a whip in his trotter." Here, we realise that during the many years that have passed, the rulers of Animal Farm have continued to learn. The pigs' power has continued to evolve, to the point where they now possess a physical weapon of oppression to uphold their power.

"'Four legs good, two legs better! Four legs good, two legs better! Four legs good, two legs better!'" The **repetitive exclamations** made by the sheep are alarming, primarily because they are a complete antithesis to the original slogan, "four legs good, two legs bad". Now, the values of the farm have shifted drastically, such that physical human traits are deemed to be synonymous with perfection.

"ALL ANIMALS ARE EQUAL BUT SOME ANIMALS ARE MORE EQUAL THAN OTHERS." Orwell's **paradoxical** rendition of one of the Seven Commandments demonstrates how totalitarian regimes assert the absolute equality of all its citizens, yet continue to designate power and privileges to certain individuals. Further, the idea of being "more equal" is illogical, thus revealing the pervasive influence of the pigs in distorting language for their own ends.

"After that it did not seem strange when next day the pigs who were supervising the work of the farm all carried whips in their trotters. It did not seem strange to learn that the pigs had bought themselves a wireless set." In spite of their previous condemnation of these items, the pigs are now welcoming these devices. The **anaphora** of the pigs engaging further in the inventions of man serves to reinforce their perception that humankind is now the new pinnacle of existence.

"Today he and his friends had visited Animal Farm and inspected every inch of it with their own eyes, and what did they find? Not only the most up-to-date methods, but a discipline and an orderliness which should be an example to all farmers everywhere." Amongst all the other drastic changes on the farm, we see that the pigs have suddenly forged a stable relationship with the neighbouring farmers, with the farmers even viewing Animal Farm as a new standard of excellence. This respect illustrates how the pigs and farmers have similar aspirations for their respective farms, thus creating a point of unity between the two parties.

"Their struggles and their difficulties were one. Was not the labour problem the same everywhere?" Orwell's **rhetorical question** further builds upon the camaraderie between the pigs and farmers, as their overlapping issues becomes a reason for them to work together.

"Hitherto the animals on the farm had had a rather foolish custom of addressing one another as 'Comrade.' This was to be suppressed." The abolition of this custom reveals the more direct approach that the pigs are taken in asserting their absolute control over the other animals, as opposed to the façade of benevolence used in previous chapters.

"That the name 'Animal Farm' had been abolished. Henceforward the farm was to be known as 'The Manor Farm' – which, he believed, was its correct and original name." The reversion of "Animal Farm" to "Manor Farm" **metaphorically** illustrates the downfall of Major's aspirations of a utopian society, as the farm regresses to its original state of oppression.

"The source of the trouble appeared to be that Napoleon and Mr. Pilkington had each played an ace of spades simultaneously." This act of deceit presents a common aspect of **characterisation** between the men and pigs, in that they are both duplicitous. Hence, Orwell continues to create worrying similarities between the two parties, setting up for the novella's finale. Contextually, this conflict characterises the Cold War, which was a period of heightened political tensions between the United States, and the Soviet Union, (and each of their allies).

"The creatures outside looked from pig to man, and from man to pig, and from pig to man again; but already it was impossible to say which was which." The ominous **denouement** of the novella establishes an indistinguishable boundary between the pigs and farmers, marking the pigs' final metamorphoses into tyrannical rulers. Much like the conventions of a fable, Orwell's conclusion didactically provides readers with an insight into the frightening perversion of human values arising from the abuse of power.

Section 4

Character Analysis

Major

Introduced as an old Middle White boar, Major is one of the most esteemed animals on the farm, responsible for fostering widespread belief in a system prioritising the wellbeing of animals. As the Prize boar of Jones, Major has been lucky enough to escape an early death, unlike his fellow animals. This has given him the opportunity to appreciate the extent to which humans have exploited animals: "I have had a long life; I have had much time for thought as I lay alone in my stall."

Major can be considered the primary engineer of change on the farm. His philosophy is most notably expressed within the opening chapter, whereby he expounds his values and desires for a world in which animals are free from oppression. Major asserts rebellion to be the key in initiating holistic change, and prompts the farm to adopt his system of thought. His song, "Beasts of England" becomes a major source of inspiration for the animals in their ensuing endeavours for change. Orwell characterises Major's principles as being an idealistic projection of society, yet asserts how these goals are unattainable due to humanity's inherent desire for power. This is something we see throughout the novella, as Major's ideals are gradually warped to benefit the pigs.

Orwell integrates the historical personalities of both **Karl Marx** and **Vladimir Lenin** in his creation of Major as a character. Marx was a German philosopher, most renowned for his 1848 composition *The Communist Manifesto*, the ideas of which formed the logical basis for revolution against capitalist systems. In a similar fashion, Lenin was a communist revolutionary who adopted Marxist ideals to lead the Bolshevik Party in the wake of the Russian Revolution. In considering this, we can see many of the ways in which Orwell incorporates the historic personages of Marx and Lenin into the character of Major, particularly their political perspectives and beliefs in rebellion as a catalyst for change.

Napoleon

Fittingly named after the ruthless dictator of France, Napoleon is described as a "large, rather fierce-looking Berkshire boar." Alongside Snowball and Squealer, Napoleon quickly establishes himself as one of the leaders of the farm shortly following Major's death, becoming responsible for the synthesis of Major's ideals into the ideology of Animalism.

Throughout the novella, Napoleon is most notably responsible for leading the pigs' gradual exploitation of the other animals in the farm. He takes advantage of the animals' ignorance to indulge in human inventions such as beds and alcohol, actions which would not have been deemed acceptable by the laws of Animalism. Furthermore, he removes the puppies from their mothers and uses them to become his private military force, killing anyone who speaks out against him.

Later in the novella, Napoleon goes on to establish trade relations with neighbouring farmers and deprives the other animals of their resources to carry out his desire to build the windmill. It gets even worse for the animals on the farm, as Napoleon eventually carries a whip and starts to walk on two legs, marking his transformation into a human. In this way, Orwell presents Napoleon as a villainous and deceitful character who not only intimidates the animals through force, but also socially exploits them for his personal gain.

The character of Napoleon is a literary representation of **Joseph Stalin,** the dictator of the Soviet Union from 1929 to 1953. He was responsible for the forced industrialisation and collectivisation of Russia through his Five-Year Plans, which subsequently resulted in the deaths of millions due to starvation and brutality. Orwell's portrayal of Stalin was deeply influenced by his contextual experiences of exploitation and class stratification in places such as England. Through Napoleon's character, Orwell expresses his concerns towards the dangers of totalitarian societies, in that leaders who hold absolute power are always looking to benefit themselves.

Snowball

In contrast to Napoleon, Snowball is characterised as a young boar who is "quicker in speech and more inventive," foregrounding his qualities of pragmatism and charisma. Despite being one of the leaders of the farm, his ongoing tensions with Napoleon eventuate with his expulsion from the farm.

Snowball has a more pro-active leadership role on the farm in comparison to Napoleon. He is the organiser of various committees dedicated to improving the farm: "He formed the Egg Production Committee for the hens, the Clean Tails League for the cows, the Wild Comrades' Re-education Committee." Additionally, Snowball is shown to be a master strategist, indicated by his prowess in directing the animals in the Battle of Cowshed. His goals are different to that of Napoleon, in that he endeavours to improve society through education and the development of new inventions, such as the windmill. Through his eloquent speeches, he is able to garner the animals' support for his vision of the farm's future, but is later chased away by Napoleon's dogs, effectively removing him from power. However, throughout the story, Snowball is shown to have a role as an invisible saboteur, allegedly taking many measures to uproot the dictatorship of Napoleon.

Snowball allegorically represents **Leon Trotsky** in his struggle for power with Stalin. As one of the leaders of the Bolshevik Party and a Commissar of War, Trotsky played an active role as leader of the Red Army. He was in constant contention with Stalin's policies as a proponent of the internationalist communist ideology 'Permanent Revolution' – the antithesis of Stalin's more nationalist 'Socialism-In-One-Country.' Following Lenin's death, Stalin eventually gained enough support to rise as leader (despite Trotsky being the assumed successor by most in the party), and Trotsky was subsequently exiled. Despite being banished, Trotsky continued to speak out against Stalin, writing an autobiography titled *M Life* that publicly condemned Stalin's lack of insight as a leader. Although not included in the novella, Trotsky was later assassinated by Ramón Mercader, an NKVD agent under Stalin's command. As such, Orwell uses the plight of Trotsky to convey the dangerous nature of tyrants such as Stalin who sought to terminate anyone who opposed to their control.

Squealer

Depicted as a "small, fat pig" with "very round cheeks, twinkling eyes, nimble movements, and a shrill voice," Squealer is another one of the pigs responsible for the conception of Animalism, alongside Snowball and Napoleon. Like Snowball, he is noted to be very persuasive, to the point where is able to "turn black into white."

Throughout the novella, Squealer primarily plays the role of fabricating excuses to alleviate the concerns of the animals. His persuasiveness enables him to justify the questionable actions of the pigs, ranging from sleeping in beds to drinking alcohol. Most notably, Squealer is able to convince the animals that Boxer was taken to hospital, despite being transported by a vehicle clearly labelled, "Horse Boiler and Glue Boiler, Willingdon." Squealer's manipulation subsequently causes the animals to question their recollection of the past, as they blindly accept the pigs' amendments to the Seven Commandments. Moreover, he is responsible for creating a cult around Napoleon, publicly touting him as the sole reason for success on the farm.

Squealer draws most parallels with the **Pravda,** a famous newspaper dedicated to the glorification of Stalin and the Soviet Union. Much like Squealer, the Pravda played an instrumental role in building upon Stalin's cult of personality and upholding his status as a powerful leader. It could also be suggested that Squealer bears some semblance to **Joseph Goebbels,** the Minister of Propaganda in Nazi Germany. Thus, Orwell uses the character of Squealer to illustrate the perversion of the truth caused by propaganda, criticising the depraved motivations of not only the USSR, but totalitarian regimes in general.

Boxer and Clover

Clover's traits as a "stout, motherly mare" are exemplified within the first chapter of the novella, where she tends to a nest of ducklings who recently lost their mother. She is considered one of Boxer's closest companions, and one of the more passionate supporters of Animalism. Whilst she is not as laborious as Boxer, Clover is shown to be more intelligent, learning the entire alphabet as opposed to Boxer, who only knows four letters. During the story, she develops a more questioning stance towards Napoleon's wrongdoings, yet continues to remain passive. One of her most compelling scenes arises in Chapter 7, in which she emotionally reflects upon the scenes of slaughter on the farm and leads the animals in a sad rendition of "Beasts of England." Clover's maternal instincts are further accentuated through her care for Boxer when he injures himself while working. Even as an old mare, Clover spreads the legacy of the Rebellion and principles of Animalism, foregrounding her persistent hope for a better future.

Alongside Clover, Boxer is a character who most ardently believes in the ideals of Animalism. Whilst described as "an enormous beast, nearly eighteen hands high," Boxer possesses a tender personality, illustrated by his remorse upon seemingly killing a stableboy: "I have no wish to take life, not even human life." He has the strongest work ethic amongst all the farm animals, as demonstrated by his maxim, "I will work harder." Through his tendency to lead by example, Boxer becomes a symbol of hope for the other animals to strive for a better future.

His lack of self-regard whilst working underscores a willingness to sacrifice for the farm. Indeed, his disposal of "the small straw hat which he wore in summer to keep the flies out of his ears" shows a readiness to suffer in order to support the causes of Animalism. However, this dedication seems to be his only answer to problems, even to the death of his comrades at the hands of Napoleon. Eventually, Boxer's health deteriorates, and he is sent to be slaughtered by Napoleon despite his loyalty to the farm.

The characters of Boxer and Clover collectively embody the **Russian proletariat** during the reign of Stalin. Boxer's enormous workload in the novella is used to convey the insurmountable labour that the working class were subjected to. In considering this, the tragic ending for Boxer metaphorically represents the sacrifice of the working class for the profit of the upper class. His tenacity further describes the basic psychology of the proletariat, who perceived work as being the sole solution to their issues.

The Farmers: Jones, Pilkington, and Frederick

Jones is initially presented as the main antagonist of the story and is the primary reason for the animals' revolution. He has apparently lost a large sum of money from a lawsuit, and as such, it has turned him into an alcoholic. Due to his heavy drinking, Jones often neglects the farm and forgets to feed the animals: "the fields were full of weeds, the buildings wanted roofing, the hedges were neglected, and the animals were underfed." Eventually, Jones is driven off the farm, and returns to re-establish control in the Battle of Cowshed, only to be sent off again. He purportedly dies in "an inebriate's home" away from the farm at the end of the novella. Jones' inebriated persona

Caricature: an imitation of a person where certain features are exaggerated.

as a **caricature** of the negligence of **Tsar Nicholas II,** the autocratic ruler of Russia prior to the Russian Revolution. The manner in which Jones neglects the farm deeply reflects the shortcomings of Nicholas II as a ruler.

Pilkington and Frederick are two other farmers who, despite their deep dislike for each other, have a collective fear of the situation on Jones' farm. They are frightened by the concept of an **autonomous** farm where the animals have absolute control, and overtly sully the reputation of the farm through lies and rumours. The men of Pilkington and Frederick's farms join forces with Jones in the Battle of Cowshed but are defeated and chased off Animal Farm. When Napoleon establishes trade relations with neighbouring farms, Pilkington and Frederick have ongoing conflicts, with each wishing to obtain timber from Napoleon. Frederick's **duplicitous** nature is revealed when he eventually trades for Napoleon's timber with a pile of counterfeit notes.

Autonomous: self-governing.

Duplicitous: deceitful or two-faced.

Frederick represents **Hitler,** whilst Pilkington represents **the governments of the West (the US and UK),** The heightened tensions between Frederick and Pilkington allegorises the political animosity between the two nations prior to WWII. Napoleon's decision to trade with Frederick characterises the **Nazi-Soviet Non-Aggression Pact.** However, Frederick's eventual betrayal of Napoleon is a stark allusion to the way in which Germany eventually opted to invade Russia in the Battle of Stalingrad.

Mollie

Mollie is introduced to audiences as a "foolish, pretty white mare." Her narcissistic personality is shown through her desires for materialistic items such as ribbons. She is a rather **anachronistic** character, in that she prioritises her individualistic values over her comrades' endeavours for freedom against Jones. During the Battle of Cowshed, she is nowhere to be seen, and is eventually found hiding in her stall. After the Rebellion, Mollie deserts the farm and is last seen with another farmer, decked in ribbons and eating sugar.

Anachronistic: something belonging to a different time period.

Mollie is a satirical representation of the **Russian nobility,** who were not receptive to the changes elicited by the Rebellion. As figures who predominantly built their wealth through capitalism, the nobles sought to retain their fortune by fleeing Russia following the Revolution and taking their prized possessions with them. They formed a part of the white émigré community, establishing their lives in other countries, such as France.

Moses

Perhaps one of the more intriguing characters in the story, Moses does not seem to play a large role in the Rebellion. Rather, he spends his time preaching about Sugarcandy Mountain, a supposed haven for all animals in the afterlife. In this way, it can be said that Moses seems to backtrack the efforts of Snowball and Napoleon by distracting the animals with premature visions of utopia. After the Rebellion, Moses disappears for a large portion of the novella, only to return to the farm with the same religious musings.

Moses represents the **Russian Orthodox Church,** which had a strong relationship with the monarchy before the Russian Revolution. In this sense, Sugarcandy Mountain draws parallels to heaven. Religion played a large role in the society of Russia under the rule of Tsar Nicholas II, as religion dictated the Tsar's divine right to rule the country. After the establishment of Communist power following the Russian Revolution, the Bolsheviks removed the influence of the Church by supporting atheism in education systems, taking ownership of church property and sending thousands of clergies to **gulags**.

Gulag: forced labour camp that many prisoners were sent to under the reign of Joseph Stalin.

Upon Moses' return later in the novel, we begin to see how the pigs continue to express their contempt for his anecdotes, but do not actively remove him from the farm. Much to the pigs' approval, Moses' claims instil a sense of hope within the animals to continue working, echoing Karl Marx's sentiments that religion "is the opium of the people." It reflects Stalin's revival of the Russian Orthodox Church in 1941 in an attempt to spark a sense of patriotism during the course of WWII.

Benjamin

Although very sparing with his words, Benjamin the donkey is naturally a cynical character, demonstrated through his passive role in the revolution and its ensuing events. Much like a donkey, he is stereotypically stubborn and adheres to his philosophy that life is inevitably riddled with struggle and grief. Throughout the story, he provides very cryptic messages to the animals: "Donkeys live a long time. None of you has ever seen a dead donkey." He seems to be the only animal who understands the motivations behind the actions of the pigs, yet continues to remain tight-lipped, for a reason that is not fully elucidated in the novella. One of the only times he intervenes is when his friend Boxer is sent to be slaughtered. In the last chapter, we see that Benjamin's observation that "life would go on as it had always gone on – that is, badly" is an accurate depiction of the future, underscoring his lack of faith in the possibility of meaningful change. Benjamin allegorises **the individuals in Russia who were aware of Stalin's oppressive policies but were averse to the idea of taking decisive action.**

Section 5

Key Themes Analysis

Before the key themes are presented, it is important to note that these themes are only a broad spectrum of ideas which are prevalent throughout the novella. In an essay, you should endeavour to explore the **main message** that the composer is attempting to convey through these themes. The purpose of an essay is to showcase your perspective about the composer's work, and so writing something such as "Orwell explores the theme of truth vs. lies" won't capture what is really being said.

Leitmotif: a recurrent theme or symbol throughout a literary text.

Power

The most obvious **leitmotif** of *Animal Farm* is that of power. It is essentially the driving force behind many of the events of the novella. Within the very first chapter, readers are positioned to witness the mistreatment of the animals by their negligent owner Farmer Jones, demonstrating an obvious imbalance of power. Embodying Karl Marx's political ideals, Major's speech to the animals serves as idealistic projection of a future where power is equally shared amongst the animals. Here, we begin to see shades of the Marxian theory of **dialectical materialism,** in which the oppressed animals are yearning for freedom.

Dialectical materialism: a Marxist term that interprets history as being shaped by a constant struggle between economic interests and class conflicts.

Indeed, the actualisation of Marx's theory emerges in the form of the animals' retaliation against Jones. They are able to finally drive him away from the farm and re-establish autonomy. Momentarily, audiences are introduced to the ending of the classic **dichotomous** story of 'good vs bad' where the protagonists challenge the power of the antagonist to establish a better world for all. Yet, this is most certainly not the case for *Animal Farm* – we see almost an immediate shift in power as the pigs are elected leaders of the farm due to their superior intellect.

Dichotomous: a division or contrast between two things that are represented as being entirely different.

Moreover, there is a noticeable struggle for power between Snowball and Napoleon, whose conflict stems from their opposing intentions: "whatever suggestion either of them made, the other could be counted on to oppose ." Even when Napoleon eventually drives Snowball away from the farm, his power over the animals is continually challenged by the latter through **espionage** – "they confessed that they had been secretly in touch with Snowball ever since his expulsion, that they had collaborated with him in destroying the windmill." Even after Jones is defeated, he along with his fellow farmers return to re-establish control over the farm in the Battle of Cowshed. Despite the expulsion of Mr. Jones, we can see that the lust for power remains quality that is prevalent across all chapters within the major characters.

Espionage: the practice of spying or using spies.

The greatest abuse of power is arguably most evident in the tyrannical dictatorship of Napoleon, paralleling Stalin's regime which led to the death of millions. This dominance is established both through physical and verbal means. Initially, the pigs assert their power under the guise of altruism, supposedly sacrificing themselves for the wellbeing of the other animals on the farm: "'You do not imagine, I hope, that we pigs are doing this in a spirit of selfishness and privilege?'" With the establishment of the animals' trust, the pigs slowly begin to build their own power through lies and rhetoric to explain questionable mishaps on the farm. Finally, we begin to see the sheer power of Napoleon in its physical manifestation of brute force. The dogs are used to assert physical dominance over the other animals, adding the factor of terror to Napoleon's rule.

Through his allegorical portrayal of Napoleon and Snowball, Orwell illustrates how humans are inherently drawn to the idea of power, revealing a mutualistic relationship between corruption and power. As complex beings, Orwell depicts how our desire to fulfil our own ambitions can often set the foundations for conflict and corrupt one's moral codes in the process.

Exploitation

Animal Farm emerges as an exposé of working-class exploitation in Soviet Russia and the subsequent perversion of freedom. Despite condemning the socialist regime established by Stalin, Orwell was actually a strong supporter of socialist policies, but believed that the Soviet Union distorted these ideals to align with their own agenda of power. Orwell's experiences of classism in Burma prompted him to champion the rights of the proletariat, a belief that essentially distinguished him as a democratic socialist.

In the novella, Orwell initially depicts the philosophy of communism as an idealistic society whereby all animals are treated equally and designated with shared workloads. Represented as Animalism within the book, the utopian visions of Major are condensed into a set of commandments, almost like the Decalogue. As promising as the farm appears to be initially, readers are positioned to gradually witness the descent of the farm into a totalitarian society, something that Orwell was vehemently against as a democratic socialist. Due to their intellectual qualities, the pigs are able to assert their authority over the other farm animals through rhetoric and deception. As a consequence, they subvert many of the previously established commandments to accommodate for their own self-indulgent desires: "All animals are equal, but some are more equal than others." It is evident that *Animal Farm* is not only a focused critique of the Soviet Union, but all totalitarian regimes in general. Orwell portrays these societies as being built upon oppression and the subjugation of the individual's spirit, a fear which manifested from his experiences of colonialism in India and Burma. He asserts that the concept of equality is based on the idea that everyone is altruistic, which is not always true as we have seen through the character of Napoleon.

Decalogue: the Ten Commandments or religious principles that dictate the ethics of those who worship God.

Manipulation

The interplay between truth and lie emerges primarily through the language of the characters within the novella. We see many examples of manipulation, particularly through Squealer.

Squealer most evidently embodies the concept of manipulation in *Animal Farm*. Throughout the story, he adopts the role as the voice of reason on the farm, justifying a large majority of the decisions made by the pigs. Much like Old Major in his speeches, Squealer uses **pathos** to compel the animals to agree with the agenda of the pigs. Yet, in the later chapters, we begin to see how this is also used as a tactic to frighten the animals into submission: "Do you know what would happen if we pigs failed in our duty? Jones would come back! Yes, Jones would come back!"

Pathos: a quality that evokes pity or sadness.

Squealer's rhetoric is additionally used to project an image of heroism for Napoleon. Mirroring Stalin's cult of personality, Napoleon is idolised as a valiant leader to the animals, and history is rewritten in a way that portrays this idea. The pigs organise parades and performances of splendour to celebrate Napoleon, subsequently creating a homogenised identity for the farm. Through manipulation alone, Squealer provides a way for the pigs to subjugate the animals and establish absolute authority over the farm. In this way, Orwell extends upon his critique of totalitarian regimes, conveying their capacity to manipulate the truth in their pursuit of power.

Hope

Hope is a major driving point for the plot of the story. It is intrinsically linked to the entire revolution, as it provides the animals with a genuine desire to elicit meaningful change to their current social landscape.

At the beginning of the novella, Old Major's dream stands as an optimistic vision of the future. His speech in Chapter 1 prompts the animals to believe that this future is achievable. Even after his death, readers can appreciate the lasting effect of his legacy, which is embodied within the anthem "Beasts of England." Throughout the story, the song stands as a lasting symbol of hope for the farm.

However, as we progress through the story, we begin to see the unravelling of Major's vision, and the subsequent loss of hope on the farm. The pigs' perversion of the Seven Commandments ultimately causes the animals to question their beliefs within the system. This is most evidently highlighted in Clover's reflections in Chapter 7, in which she is faced with the heart retching loss of a peaceful future she had once envisaged for all animals. In particular, this scene is significant, as Clover's desires allow audiences to deeply empathise with her character. Through characters such as Clover, we begin to appreciate the value of freedom and individualism.

However, audiences are given insight into the loss of hope through the pigs' rise to power. In the latter chapters of the novella, false hope is used as a tool of oppression: "he proved to them in detail that they had more oats, more hay, more turnips than they had had in Jones' day, that they worked shorter hours." Moses' religious musings about Sugarcandy Mountain similarly provide the animals with a false hope that their lives can still be better, but realistically it does nothing but pacify the animals. Ultimately, the tragic ending of the pigs seamlessly transforming into humans marks a cyclical process in which hope is created and destroyed as a result of the desire for power.

Ignorance

The quality of ignorance is one that is prominent within many of the animals on the farm. Throughout the story, the rest of the farm continue to believe in the supposedly noble motivations of the pigs, despite the obvious signs of their corruption.

The sheep are one such group who demonstrate an inability to think for themselves. Adhering to their stereotypes, the sheep blindly follow the orders of the pigs. Throughout the story, they seem to have no meaningful contribution to the discussion between the farm animals. Their only responsibility seems to involve repeating the simple maxim, "Four legs good, two legs bad!" Eventually, when the pigs take over the farm, the sheep are taught to revise their phrase into "four legs good, two legs better!" and they are able to do so without any hesitation.

The other animals of the farm demonstrate a level of ignorance, as they continue to blindly believe anything the pigs tell them. They seem to think that the pigs are undoubtedly acting in the best interests of the farm. As such, they are willing to accept the unfair rationing of food supplies and are erroneously led to believe that Snowball was a saboteur of the farm. Even when the pigs carry out horrific acts of violence, the animals refuse to believe that the system is corrupt, instead opting to blame it on themselves, as exemplified by Boxer: "I would not have believed that such things could happen on our farm. It must be due to some fault in ourselves. The solution, as I see it, is to work harder." Eventually, the animals' inability to discern the corruption within their farm leads to the gradual takeover by the pigs.

Orwell suggests that the oppression of the animals was not only caused by the pigs' manipulative tendencies, but also by the foolishness of the animals. This becomes an allegorical translation of Orwell's perceptions towards the Russian society. Orwell criticised the concept of socialism in England, whereby he felt the lower classes lacked the ideological understanding of socialism they adhered to.

Section 6

Structural Features Analysis

Animal Farm is structured as a **fable** or **allegory,** narrated across ten chapters. You may have noticed that the novel is fairly easy to read, especially compared to other literary classics like Victorian novels or Shakespeare! This is because Orwell deliberately uses simple and direct language – a common characteristic of fables – to make the story accessible to readers of all ages and backgrounds. However, beneath this simplicity lies a complex critique of power and corruption.

The storyline is structured as a **circular narrative** – that is, the conclusion of the novella is no different to the opening of the story. In the end, the animals find themselves in a similar situation of oppression, only now it is under the reign of Napoleon confined to the **setting** of a farm, a **microcosm** for broader society. As the pigs gradually assume power, the setting of the farm changes. It starts as a place of hope and freedom following the rebellion but becomes increasingly oppressive under Napoleon's rule. These changes in the farm's atmosphere reflect the shift in political power and the corruption of the original revolutionary ideals.

Microcosm: a small concept that represents or encapsulates the characteristics of something bigger.

The novella is also intended to be a **satirical allegory.** Drawing upon the conventions of a fable, Orwell incorporates a moral lesson to the story by conveying the political fallacies of totalitarianism. Rather than write a biographical piece about the Stalin and the Soviet Union's wrongdoings, Orwell instead chose to write a story about farm animals with each one representing specific human traits of historical figures. For example:

- **Napoleon** represents Joseph Stalin.
- **Snowball** represents Leon Trotsky.
- **Old Major** represents Karl Marx and/or Vladimir Lenin.
- **Mr Jones** represents Tsar Nicholas II.
- **Boxer** the hardworking horse represents the loyal but exploited working class.
- **Squealer** represents the state media.
- **Moses** the raven represents organised religion.
- **Mollie** represents the upper class who were content under the Tsar's rule.
- **Benjamin:** indecisive, passive bystanders to Stalin's rule.

- **The pigs** represent the ruling class under Stalin.
- **The dogs** represent the secret police enforcers (NKVD).
- **The hens** represent the peasants.
- **The sheep** represent the subservient masses.

The novel highlights the development of a hierarchy on the farm, starting with the pigs claiming leadership and eventually exploiting the other animals. This structure mirrors the development of class stratification in totalitarian societies, illustrating how power can corrupt revolutionary movements. To an extent, this simplifies the horrific actions of the Soviet Union under Stalin. However, its form as a fable makes it more accessible to a wider audience, allowing for more people to appreciate the messages intertwined within the story.

As another generic staple of fables, Orwell adopts a third person perspective to describe the events on the farm. The narrator is **omniscient**, but at the same time, they display a level of ignorance towards many of the strange occurrences on the farm. Rather than explaining many of these incidents, the narrator opts to comment and provide basic observations: "About this time there was a strange incident which hardly anyone was able to understand." In doing so, Orwell establishes a sense of **dramatic irony** – readers are aware of what is happening but are the only ones to have this knowledge.

Omniscient: all-knowing; a narrator who has an awareness of everything that is happening in the story.

This also extends to the readers' awareness of how slogans like "four legs good, two legs bad" and "all animals are equal, but some animals are more equal than others" can be understood as **propaganda.** Squealer's persuasive speeches, filled with manipulation and half-truths, also foreshadow the pigs' eventual betrayal of the other animals. By foreshadowing these betrayals, Orwell demonstrates how leaders can gradually erode freedom under the guise of serving the common good.

Literary features

Structural feature	Analysis and purpose
Fable	This genre allows Orwell to portray complex political ideas in a simple and relatable way. It also enables him to critique human behaviour through the actions of animals, which provides distance from real-world political figures.
Allegory	The story is a symbolic narrative in which characters represent broader sociopolitical ideas, paralleling the events of the Russian Revolution and the rise of Stalinism. Through allegory, Orwell critiques totalitarian regimes, the betrayal of revolutionary ideals, and the manipulation of power.
Circular narrative	This creates a sense of inevitability and inescapability, suggesting that the pigs were always going to abuse their power and become tyrants.
Setting	The small, rural farm in England serves as a microcosm for the world and, more specifically, the Soviet Union. The simplicity of the farm setting helps universalise the themes of the novel. It also mirrors the isolationist policies often adopted by totalitarian regimes.
Allegory	Each character serves as a symbol for larger social and political forces.
Omniscient narration	The all-knowing narrator grants readers access to a deeper understanding than the characters have, creating an ironic gap between what the animals think and what we know is really happening.
Dramatic irony	The animals on the farm remain unaware of the pigs' betrayal, but the reader can clearly see how the pigs are exploiting them. This dramatic irony heightens the reader's awareness of the corruption of the pigs and underscores the theme of exploitation.
Propaganda slogans	These slogans represent the manipulative power of language and propaganda. They are used by the pigs to control the other animals and justify their actions, mirroring how political regimes manipulate language to control the populace.

Symbols

Symbol	Meaning	Analysis
The farm	The Soviet Union under Communist rule	Through this symbol, Orwell critiques the oppressive nature of totalitarian states and the betrayal of revolutionary ideals.
The windmill	Manipulation of the working class – initially a project for the common good, but becomes a tool for the pigs to consolidate power	The windmill symbolises empty promises of progress that are exploited by those in power to maintain control over the masses.
Seven Commandments	Principles of equality and a means of maintaining order	The gradual changes emphasise the erosion of equality and the manipulation of laws by those in power to suit their own interests.
The pigs	The ruling class, specifically Stalin and his regime	Orwell uses the pigs to highlight the ways in which those in power often betray the principles they originally stood for, becoming indistinguishable from the oppressive regimes they replaced.
Milk and apples	Riches, wealth, and privilege	The pigs feel entitlement to these 'spoils of war' and claim ownership of them at the expense of the other animals.
Old Major's skull	Appropriating the past to give legitimacy to the new regime	Napoleon digs up the skull and uses it as a symbol of fealty, though later abandons this which suggests he is also jettisoning any principles he deems inconvenient
Jones' rifle	Animal victory over humans	The animals claim this rifle after the Battle of the Cowshed when the humans are forced to retreat. Thus, it is a trophy they use to celebrate their success.

Section 7

Quote Bank

Power

Quote	Speaker	Chapter
"Now, comrades, what is the nature of this life of ours? Let us face it: our lives are miserable, laborious, and short"	Major	1
"No animal in England knows the meaning of happiness or leisure after he is a year old. No animal in England is free."	Major	1
"And you, Clover, where are those four foals you bore, who should have been the support and pleasure of your old age? Each was sold at a year old — you will never see one of them again."	Major	1
"Never listen when they tell you that Man and the animals have a common interest, that the prosperity of the one is the prosperity of the others. It is all lies. Man serves the interests of no creature except himself."	Major	1
"Snowball and Napoleon were by far the most active in the debates. But it was noticed that these two were never in agreement: whatever suggestion either of them made, the other could be counted on to oppose it."	Narrator	3
"The other farmers sympathised in principle, but they did not at first give him much help. At heart, each of them was secretly wondering whether he could not somehow turn Jones' misfortune to his own advantage."	Narrator	4
"'No sentimentality, comrade!' cried Snowball from whose wounds the blood was still dripping. 'War is war. The only good human being is a dead one.'"	Snowball	4

Quote	Speaker	Chapter
"These two disagreed at every point where disagreement was possible. If one of them suggested sowing a bigger acreage with barley, the other was certain to demand a bigger acreage of oats"	Narrator	5
"At the Meetings Snowball often won over the majority by his brilliant speeches, but Napoleon was better at canvassing support for himself in between times"	Narrator	5
"They kept close to Napoleon. It was noticed that they wagged their tails to him in the same way as the other dogs had been used to do to Mr. Jones."	Narrator	5
"'This traitor has crept here under cover of night and destroyed our work of nearly a year. Comrades, here and now I pronounce the death sentence upon Snowball.'"	Napoleon	6
"When he did emerge, it was in a ceremonial manner, with an escort of six dogs who closely surrounded him and growled if anyone came too near."	Narrator	7
"One Sunday morning Squealer announced that the hens, who had just come in to lay again, must surrender their eggs. Napoleon had accepted, through Whymper, a contract for four hundred eggs a week."	Narrator	7
"Napoleon acted swiftly and ruthlessly. He ordered the hens' rations to be stopped, and decreed that any animal giving so much as a grain of corn to a hen should be punished by death."	Narrator	7
"When they had finished their confession, the dogs promptly tore their throats out, and in a terrible voice Napoleon demanded whether any other animal had anything to confess."	Narrator	7
"He carried a whip in his trotter."	Narrator	10
"He believed that he was right in saying that the lower animals on Animal Farm did more work and received less food than any animals in the county."	Narrator	10
"Hitherto the animals on the farm had had a rather foolish custom of addressing one another as 'Comrade.' This was to be suppressed."	Narrator	10

Exploitation

Quote	Speaker	Chapter
"So the animals trooped down to the hayfield to begin the harvest, and when they came back in the evening it was noticed that the milk had disappeared."	Narrator	2
"He announced that from now on the Sunday-morning Meetings would come to an end. They were unnecessary, he said, and wasted time."	Narrator	5
"The four young pigs who had protested when Napoleon abolished the Meetings raised their voices timidly, but they were promptly silenced by a tremendous growling from the dogs."	Narrator	5
"And when, some days afterwards, it was announced that from now on the pigs would get up an hour later in the mornings than the other animals, no complaint was made about that either"	Narrator	6
"Muriel read the Commandment for her. It ran: 'No animal shall kill any other animal without cause.' Somehow or other, the last two words had slipped out of the animals' memory."	Narrator	7
"Even in the farmhouse, it was said, Napoleon inhabited separate apartments from the others. He took his meals alone, with two dogs to wait upon him, and always ate from the Crown Derby dinner service which had been in the glass cupboard in the drawing-room."	Narrator	8
"He was always referred to in formal style as 'our Leader, Comrade Napoleon,' and this pigs liked to invent for him such titles as Father of All Animals, Terror of Mankind, Protector of the Sheep-fold, Ducklings' Friend, and the like."	Narrator	8
"He personally congratulated the animals on their achievement, and announced that the mill would be named Napoleon Mill."	Narrator	8
"Napoleon had created a new decoration, the Order of the Green Banner, which he had conferred upon himself."	Narrator	8

"By the evening of that day Napoleon was back at work, and on the next day it was learned that he had instructed Whymper to purchase in Willingdon some booklets on brewing and distilling."	Narrator	8
"At the foot of the end wall of the big barn, where the Seven Commandments were written, there lay a ladder broken in two pieces. Squealer, temporarily stunned, was sprawling beside it, and near at hand there lay a lantern, a paint- brush, and an overturned pot of white paint."	Narrator	8
"Rations, reduced in December, were reduced again in February, and lanterns in the stalls were forbidden to save Oil. But the pigs seemed comfortable enough, and in fact were putting on weight if anything."	Narrator	9
"And the news soon leaked out that every pig was now receiving a ration of a pint of beer daily, with half a gallon for Napoleon himself, which was always served to him in the Crown Derby soup tureen."	Narrator	9
"But no warm mash appeared, and on the following Sunday it was announced that from now onwards all barley would be reserved for the pigs."	Narrator	9
"Afterwards there were recitations of poems composed in Napoleon's honour."	Narrator	9
"Forward in the name of the Rebellion. Long live Animal Farm! Long live Comrade Napoleon! Napoleon is always right.' Those were his very last words, comrades."	Squealer	9
"No one stirred in the farmhouse before noon on the following day, and the word went round that from somewhere or other the pigs had acquired the money to buy themselves another case of whisky."	Squealer	9
"'Four legs good, two legs better! Four legs good, two legs better! Four legs good, two legs better!'"	Sheep	10
"Some of them had five chins, some had four, some had three. But what was it that seemed to be melting and changing?"	Clover	10

Manipulation

Quote	Speaker	Chapter
"He was a brilliant talker, and when he was arguing some difficult point he had a way of skipping from side to side and whisking his tail which was somehow very persuasive. The others said of Squealer that he could turn black into white."	Narrator	2
"'Comrades!' he cried. 'You do not imagine, I hope, that we pigs are doing this in a spirit of selfishness and privilege? Many of us actually dislike milk and apples"	Squealer	3
"'Do you know what would happen if we pigs failed in our duty? Jones would come back! Yes, Jones would come back!'"	Squealer	3
"So it was agreed without further argument that the milk and the windfall apples (and also the main crop of apples when they ripened) should be reserved for the pigs alone."	Narrator	3
"'No one believes more firmly than Comrade Napoleon that all animals are equal. He would be only too happy to let you make your decisions for yourselves. But sometimes you might make the wrong decisions, comrades, and then where should we be?'"	Squealer	5
"'One false step, and our enemies would be upon us. Surely, comrades, you do not want Jones back?'"	Squealer	5
"Had not these been among the earliest resolutions passed at that first triumphant Meeting after Jones was expelled? All the animals remembered passing such resolutions: or at least they thought that they remembered it."	Narrator	6
"'Are you certain that this is not something that you have dreamed, comrades? Have you any record of such a resolution? Is it written down anywhere?'"	Squealer	6

"'And do you not remember, too, that it was just at that moment, when panic was spreading and all seemed lost, that Comrade Napoleon sprang forward with a cry of 'Death to Humanity!' and sank his teeth in Jones' leg? Surely you remember that, comrades?' exclaimed Squealer, frisking from side to side."	Squealer	7
"The animals saw no reason to disbelieve him, especially as they could no longer remember very clearly what conditions had been like before the Rebellion."	Narrator	8
"A too rigid equality in rations, Squealer explained, would have been contrary to the principles of Animalism."	Narrator	9
"For the time being, certainly, it had been found necessary to make a readjustment of rations (Squealer always spoke of it as a 'readjustment,' never as a 'reduction')"	Narrator	9
"There was nothing with which they could compare their present lives: they had nothing to go upon except Squealer's lists of figures, which invariably demonstrated that everything was getting better and better."	Narrator	10

Ignorance

Quote	Speaker	Chapter
"The stupidest questions of all were asked by Mollie, the white mare. The very first question she asked Snowball was: 'Will there still be sugar after the Rebellion?'"	Narrator	2
"The birds did not understand Snowball's long words, but they accepted his explanation."	Narrator	3
"On every kind of pretext she would run away from work and go to the drinking pool, where she would stand foolishly gazing at her own reflection in the water."	Narrator	5
"Gradually the plans grew into a complicated mass of cranks and cog-wheels, covering more than half the floor, which the other animals found completely unintelligible but very impressive."	Narrator	5
"And from then on he adopted the maxim, 'Napoleon is always right,' in addition to his private motto of 'I will work harder.'"	Boxer	5
"The animals were not certain what the word meant, but Squealer spoke so persuasively, and the three dogs who happened to be with him growled so threateningly, that they accepted his explanation without further questions."	Narrator	5
"'Ah, that is different!' said Boxer. 'If Comrade Napoleon says it, it must be right.'"	Boxer	7
"'I do not understand it. I would not have believed that such things could happen on our farm. It must be due to some fault in ourselves. The solution, as I see it, is to work harder.'"	Boxer	7
"'Fools! Fools!' shouted Benjamin, prancing round them and stamping the earth with his small hoofs. 'Fools! Do you not see what is written on the side of that van?'"	Benjamin	9
"There was, as Squealer was never tired of explaining, endless work in the supervision and organisation of the farm. Much of this work was of a kind that the other animals were too ignorant to understand."	Narrator	10

Hope

Quote	Speaker	Chapter
"But is this simply part of the order of nature? Is it because this land of ours is so poor that it cannot afford a decent life to those who dwell upon it? No, comrades, a thousand times no!"	Major	1
"Weak or strong, clever or simple, we are all brothers. No animal must ever kill any other animal. All animals are equal."	Major	1
"There, comrades, is the answer to all our problems. It is summed up in a single word – Man. Man is the only real enemy we have."	Major	1
"What then must we do? Why, work night and day, body and soul, for the overthrow of the human race! That is my message to you, comrades: Rebellion!"	Major	1
"All men are enemies. All animals are comrades."	Major	1
"And then, after a few preliminary tries, the whole farm burst out into Beasts of England in tremendous unison."	Narrator	1
"He claimed to know of the existence of a mysterious country called Sugarcandy Mountain, to which all animals went when they died."	Narrator	2
"Bulls which had always been tractable suddenly turned savage, sheep broke down hedges and devoured the clover, cows kicked the pail over, hunters refused their fences and shot their riders on to the other side."	Narrator	4
"In glowing sentences he painted a picture of Animal Farm as it might be when sordid labour was lifted from the animals' backs. His imagination had now run far beyond chaff-cutters and turnip-slicers. Electricity, he said, could operate threshing machines, ploughs, harrows, rollers, and reapers and binders, besides supplying every stall with its own electric light, hot and cold water, and an electric heater."	Narrator	5

"The enormous difference that would be made in their lives when the sails were turning and the dynamos running — when they thought of all this, their tiredness forsook them and they gambolled round and round the windmill, uttering cries of triumph."	Narrator	8
"He even claimed to have been there on one of his higher flights, and to have seen the everlasting fields of clover and the linseed cake and lump sugar growing on the hedges."	Narrator	9
"Their lives now, they reasoned, were hungry and laborious; was it not right and just that a better world should exist somewhere else?"	Narrator	9
"It would be the first time that he had had leisure to study and improve his mind. He intended, he said, to devote the rest of his life to learning the remaining twenty-two letters of the alphabet."	Narrator	9
"And yet the animals never gave up hope. More, they never lost, even for an instant, their sense of honour and privilege in being members of Animal Farm."	Narrator	10
"None of the old dreams had been abandoned. The Republic of the Animals which Major had foretold, when the green fields of England should be untrodden by human feet, was still believed in."	Narrator	10

Section 8

Sample Essays

Essay One

QUESTION: Discuss the portrayal of power in George Orwell's *Animal Farm*.

ESSAY	COMMENTS
INTRODUCTION Texts are fundamentally constructs that endeavour to explore and critique the paradigms of their contextual climates.[1] George Orwell's 1945 novella *Animal Farm* encapsulates the contextual concerns of his time by conveying the loss of equality which he perceived to be prevalent across totalitarian regimes. Reflecting the repressive Stalinist ideologies of his context, Orwell further explores the absolute subjugation of the human spirit arising from the abuse of power by despotic leaders.[2] To a large extent, Orwell's authorial perspectives are shaped by the events of the post WWII era, as he provides a harrowing contextual insight into the abandonment of essential human values facilitated by humanity's inherent desires for power.[3]	1. I like to begin my introductions with a general statement relating to the essay question. It allows me to transition more easily into the ideas that I will be talking about. Some people like to directly begin with a thesis statement, and this is fine as well. Just do whatever you are comfortable with! 2. These next two sentences explain the specific ideas that I will be talking about in the body paragraphs. There shouldn't be much storytelling, just a quick overview of what will be explored (almost like a topic sentence). 3. This is the bulk of my thesis statement expanding upon the essay question. Try to do more than provide a direct answer to the question. A good thesis should incorporate a rationale or reason behind why you agree/disagree with the question.

PARAGRAPH 1

Through its creation of a dystopian state, *Animal Farm* actualises Orwell's contextual fears of totalitarianism to explore the perversion of equality amidst a hostile political landscape.[4] Reflecting Stalin's Five Year Plans,[5] Napoleon's high modality claim, "the needs of the windmill must override anything else" metaphorically condemns the individual to a servant of the state, foregrounding the devaluation of the human identity within totalitarian regimes. Further, his eponymous branding of the windmill as "Napoleon Mill" denotes a profound sense of narcissism that deeply parallels the pervasive nature of Stalin's cult of personality. This superiority complex displayed by Napoleon becomes a focal point of critique for Orwell, as he highlights the intrinsically despotic tendencies of dictators such as Stalin and Hitler. The paradoxical maxim "all animals are equal but some animals are more equal than others" presents a logical fallacy that displays Orwell's concerns towards the totalising influence of tyrannical leaders in manipulating language to align with their own agenda of power.[6] It forges a society where the younger pigs are "discouraged from playing with the other young animals", revealing a sense of Marxian Entfremdung caused by the pigs' progressive abuse of power. By extension, the irony within Napoleon's claim that "true happiness... lay in working hard and living frugally"[7] underpins the exploitation of the working class, in which they are relegated to a state of modest labour in contrast to the lavish lifestyles of the elite. This repressed lifestyle presents to responders a dramatic loss of freedom and happiness that becomes deeply reminiscent of life within the Gulags.

4. A topic sentence should focus on the idea that you are going to explore and should have a strong link to the essay question. It gives the reader/marker a clear idea of where you are headed with this paragraph.

5. A focus on the specific contextual events during Stalin's reign shows that you have a deep understanding of the text. It also demonstrates a high level of thought in your interpretation of the novella.

6. As a general rule, I like to follow a structure of TEE when presenting analysis of a quote: T (technique), E (evidence), E (explain).

7. To keep the flow of an essay, I like to use shorter quotes so that the sentences don't become too tedious to read. Here, I have used ellipsis (the three dots) to indicate that I have excluded a small part of the quote which I thought was not needed. Chop and change quotes whenever you need to, just so long as it still makes sense and retains its meaning.

The inclusion of the rhetorical question, "was not the labour problem the same everywhere?" creates an ominous point of similarity between the pigs and the farmers, collectively characterising them as oppressors of their respective farms. It contextualises Orwell's perception towards the events of the Tehran Conference, as he critiques the eventual political unity between the USSR and the West. As such, Orwell reflects upon the extremist ideologies of his time to convey the diminution of equality and human dignity within a debilitating political landscape.[8]

PARAGRAPH 2

In his projection of society's decline under totalitarianism, Orwell draws upon the tragic plight of the characters to elucidate the struggle caused by humanity's myopic pursuit for power.[9] The use of asyndeton in "they slept on straw, they drank from the pool, they laboured in the field" establishes the banality of life under the reign of the pigs, foregrounding this repressed lifestyle as the quotidian for the animals. Yet, Orwell's personification in "starvation seemed to stare them in the face" concurrently highlights the animals' intense struggle for survival on the farm, contextualising the Great Famine elicited by Stalin's plans for collectivisation. Reflecting the Kulak's rise against Stalin's policies, the hens' revolution emerges as an innate desire for change, yet its tragic end in "nine hens had died in the meantime" symbolically reinforces the transience of rebellion against an overwhelming totalitarian state.

8. It is always good to end a body paragraph with a brief statement that re-iterates the paragraph's main focus and how this relates to the essay question.
9. A topic sentence should clearly outline an idea about power rather than stating something along the lines of "Orwell's *Animal Farm* explores the idea of power."

Further, the rhetorical question, "was it not right and just that a better world should exist somewhere else?" encapsulates a sentiment of yearning, underscoring the small sense of hope that drives the animals' desire to endure. In this way, Orwell provides a harrowing image of disempowerment that reinforces his critique of the bourgeoning hubristic motivations of his context.[10] Likewise, the dramatic irony in the pigs orchestrating Boxer's death to "buy themselves another case of whiskey" serves to further illustrate the way in which the animals are devalued to the point of becoming interchangeable for hedonistic luxuries. Such compassionless acts ultimately reveal a dramatic manipulation of hope and freedom that validates Benjamin's aphoristic claim of "hunger, hardship, and disappointment being... the unalterable law of life." Drawing upon the conventions of dystopian literature,[11] Orwell utilises the tragic denouement of *Animal Farm* to contextually highlight the extinguishment of the human spirit in the face of totalitarian control.

CONCLUSION

Ultimately,[12] Orwell's *Animal Farm* responds to the concerns of the post WWII era through its apocalyptic vision of totalitarian control driven by the inherent desire for power. In allegorising the plight of the animals, Orwell draws upon his own zeitgeist to reveal the deeply tragic loss of human heritage within these dehumanising political environments, utilising the form of a fable as a conduit for his didactic message.

10. Throughout my body paragraphs, I like to incorporate a sentence that re-emphasises my stance towards the essay question, just to remind the marker.
11. Although the essay question doesn't specifically mention it, a brief consideration of the text's form shows a deeper understanding of the text as a whole.
12. Conclusions should be a summary of the messages which have already been stated in the previous paragraphs. There should be nothing new for the reader to learn. Keep it short and sweet, (less than 80 words is usually ideal) and answer the question once more.

Essay Two

QUESTION: George Orwell's *Animal Farm* is an allegory for authoritarianism. To what extent do you agree?

ESSAY	COMMENTS
INTRODUCTION George Orwell's 1945 novella *Animal Farm* continues to retain its relevance to contemporary audiences due to its enduring examination of control and manipulation. The novella illustrates the absolute indoctrination of society to extremist ideologies bearing semblance to those of Stalin and Hitler, demonstrating the destructive influence that this can have upon the individual's identity. Moreover, through its depiction of a world afflicted by contradictions and lies, Orwell displays the role of language in perpetuating the manipulative tendencies of despotic leaders.[1] In this way, Orwell draws upon the events of his own post-WWII context[2] to create a dystopian projection of society, highlighting the loss of human heritage within controlling authoritarian landscapes.	1. I have taken two different approaches to control in the text. The first is control through indoctrination, and the second is control through the manipulation of language and truth. 2. Referring to the authorial context is a great way to support your discussion and show your assessor that you understand the broader zeitgeist in which the novella was written.

PARAGRAPH 1

Through its treatment of control, Orwell's *Animal Farm* reveals the insurmountable influence of despotic regimes upon all dimensions of an individual's existence. Resonant of the Moscow Show Trials, Orwell's macabre imagery in "a pile of corpses lying before Napoleon's feet and the air was heavy with the smell of blood" underscores contextual concerns about the disempowering nature of absolute control in which "loyalty and obedience" are valued over the sanctity of life. Furthermore, Squealer's rhetorical question, "surely you remember that, comrades?" foregrounds the state's control over psychological dimensions, to the point where memory no longer becomes a valid source of history. The absence of truth within Orwell's dystopian society subsequently creates a world where the animals have "nothing with which they could compare their present lives," underscoring the complete social indoctrination of society. The pigs' persistent revisionism, evidenced in the sheep's new maxim, "Four legs good, two legs better!" demonstrates an ability to shift societal orthodoxy, deeply paralleling Stalin's manipulation of mass media to create an idolised perception of himself. In doing so, Orwell prompts contemporary readers to consider the role of the media in shaping attitudes within their own societies.[4] In capturing this totality, Minimus' song, "Animal Farm, Animal Farm, Never through me shalt thou come to harm!" further places a heightened focus on the wellbeing of the state, with the undertones of sacrifice demeaning the individual to a martyr.

3. Using transitional words such as "furthermore" or "moreover" etc. helps to maintain the fluidity of an essay and also helps in presenting your ideas in a clear and logical manner.

4. This sentence is a brief comment about how this form of control through media remains relevant to our modern society, helping us to better understand the way in which the idea of control is presented in *Animal Farm.*

By extension, the exhibitions of extravagance in the Spontaneous Demonstrations coupled with "poems recited in Napoleon's honour" symbolically elucidate the pervasive influence of the ruling class in defining the identity and values of the animals as a whole. Thus, Orwell presents a dramatic loss of freedom that becomes synonymous with the animals' struggles to affirm a cohesive sense of identity within a controlling society.

PARAGRAPH 2

The manipulation of language in *Animal Farm* ultimately becomes a conduit[5] through which Orwell critically evaluates the deceitful nature of despotic leaders and their propensities to distort the truth. Allegorically emulating the USSR's gross perversion of Communist ideals, the pigs' adjustment of the Seven Commandments in "No animal shall kill any other animal without cause" symbolically elucidates the subtle way in which language is altered to align with the egotistical intentions of the pigs. Furthermore, Squealer's rhetorical assertions, "Do you know what would happen if we pigs failed in our duty? Jones would come back!" underpins the pigs' use of fear[6] as a means to achieve subjugation. It constructs a society where the animals "work like slaves," the simile ultimately epitomising the loss of hope and freedom within a world afflicted by contradictions. Paralleling the USSR's misrepresentation of statistics, Squealer's accumulation of fabricated claims, "they worked shorter hours, that their drinking water was of better quality, that they lived longer" demonstrates how hope is utilised to uphold the animals' morale, even within a harrowing social landscape.

5. This is a great word to describe the nature of the text and its function as part of Orwell's authorial intent

6. Throughout this paragraph, the evidence is used to show the *different ways* in which language is used to exert control (e.g. fear, false hope, etc.).

Moreover, it symbolises Orwell's recognition of language[7] as the primary tool of oppression endorsed by totalitarian regimes across the 20th century. The glorified epithets of Napoleon in "Father of All Animals, Terror of Mankind, Protector of the Sheepfold" convey the pigs' efforts to creates a dramatised image of Napoleon as an almighty leader, similarly reflecting the actions of the Pravda in controlling Stalin's cult of personality. Orwell's construction of Napoleon as a deity to the animals ultimately serves to illustrate his fears of a world where language is utilised to distort the ideals of truth and equality. Hence, Orwell examines the capacity of language to blur the boundaries between truth and lie in his critique towards the manipulative tendencies of totalitarian regimes.

CONCLUSION
As such, Orwell utilises a dystopian setting to heighten the audience's understanding towards the pervasive nature of control within his own context. This control manifests itself not only through social repression, but also through the manipulation of language. In this way, Orwell's *Animal Farm* shares insightful representations into the unjust brutality and corruption of the post-WWII totalitarian regimes, revealing the subsequent deprivation of meaningful human values arising from such control.[8]

7. Here is a contextual link explaining how the manipulation of language was relevant to Orwell's time.

8. This is a very strong conclusion that ties together the different threads of our argument.

Essay Three

QUESTION: To what extent does *Animal Farm* endorse the notion of hope for the future?

ESSAY	COMMENTS
INTRODUCTION The enduring value of literature lies within their capacity to provide perspectives towards essential human values which continues to resonate with contemporary readers. This idea is particularly evident within George Orwell's *Animal Farm*[1] (1945), which reacts to the uprising of totalitarianism in its portrayal of hope within an oppressive world. In depicting the struggle of the animals, Orwell explores the significance of hope in upholding the integrity of the human spirit. Yet, in response to the oppressive nature of Orwell's context, the novella culminates in a complete decimation of hope, highlighting the perversion of human values by despotic leaders such as Stalin and Hitler.[2] Therefore, despite its publication in the 20th century, Orwell's *Animal Farm* captures an essential aspect of the human condition that heightens readers' understandings towards the value of hope across changing contextual paradigms.	1. In the introduction, it is convention to always introduce the text and the full name of the author and the text before using shorter terms such as 'Orwell.' 2. The body paragraphs will be presenting two polarising perspectives of hope that are present in the novella.

PARAGRAPH 1

Orwell's *Animal Farm* captures the essence of human heritage through its depiction of hope and its potential to elicit meaningful change within society. Mirroring the plight of Russia's working class under Tsarist autocracy, Major's macabre conceptualisation of life as "misery and slavery" metaphorically highlights the necessity of hope, in that without it, individuals are subsequently relegated to a state of continual depression. His cumulative listing in "this single farm of ours would support a dozen horses, twenty cows, hundreds of sheep" instils a sense of hope[3] within the animals by creating a vision of collective prosperity that propagates the Marxist model of communism. In this way, Major's rhetorical question, "why then, do we continue in this miserable condition?" serves as a vehement rejection of the current norms of life, projecting rebellion as the key to profound change in society. To a large extent, it reflects the ensuing social disillusionment stemming from Russia's large losses in the aftermath of WWI. Thus, the anthem Beasts of England stands as a symbol of hope for the animals to pursue a better life, with its intimations of rebellion foregrounding Marx's theory of permanent revolution. Reflecting the historical traits of[3] Boxer emerges as an archetype of the working-class citizen, characterised primarily by his unrelenting work ethic and his terse maxim, "I will work harder." His persona as the "admiration of everybody" thus reveals his role as a symbol of belief for the animals, enabling them to persist in their efforts for the farm.

3. Remember that although identifying literary features within the novella can be useful, your focus should always be on *explaining* evidence and linking it to your argument. Don't simply make remarks that point out structural devices without following it up with a sentence like this that recognises the intended effect for readers.
4. Again, references to specific events and historical personalities demonstrates a heightened appreciation of the text. Doing research is important to reinforce your understanding of the novella's storyline and characters.

Ultimately, the repetitive exclamation "yes it was theirs – everything that they could see was theirs!" represents the destabilisation of the old dictatorial system, illustrating the potential of hope in holistically fashioning an ideal society for all. In exploring the idea of hope, Orwell draws upon the intrinsic traits of humanity to prompt readers to empathise with the characters of *Animal Farm* in their endeavours to pursue a better life.[5]

PARAGRAPH 2

Yet, on the opposing side of the spectrum, Orwell uses the ensuing struggle of the animals to explore the fractured ideals of hope within a world which has transcended human compassion.[6] Echoing the mindset of the Russian cynics,[7] Benjamin's comment, "life would go on as it had always gone on – that is, badly" adopts a fatalistic worldview that foreshadows the tragic fate facilitated by the animals' constant pushes for change. Likewise, Boxer's question, "what victory?" encapsulates a melancholic sentiment that reflects the social turmoil arising from the events of WWII. In this way, Orwell utilises the visceral image of the "weary and bleeding" animals to ultimately reveal the dehumanising impact of war caused by the vices of totalitarian leaders, and the diminishing effect on hope for those involved. Clover's valorised memory of "grass and the bursting hedges were gilded by the level rays of the sun" therefore emerges as a metaphor for her innate yearning to retain a sense of hope through a meaningful reconnection with the physical landscape.

5. By the end of your paragraph, you should be ready to 'zoom out' and make a broader comment about what Orwell is saying about society, or what he is attempting to evoke in his readers. This also makes for a much stronger final sentence that links your discussion and the core of the prompt to the overarching purpose of the text.

6. Here, we present a more complex perspective on the prompt and adding sophistication to our contention.

7. This is another subtle integration of our background research; remember that your marker doesn't want to read a massive information dump! Always focus on the set text and just make quick references like this to help add credence to your argument. The vast majority of your essay should be focused exclusively on the novella in order to secure your marks.

The undertones of stasis in "their life, so far as they knew, was as it had always been" subsequently highlights the banality of existence and the lack of direction on the farm due to the oppressive dictatorship of Napoleon. Thus, Orwell presents to readers a tragic vision of loss that thereby heightens their contextual understanding towards the need to retain essential human values such as freedom and hope.[8] Benjamin's aphoristic claim of "hunger, hardship, and disappointment being... the unalterable law of life" presents a Predeterministic[9] worldview towards the inevitable struggle stemming from authoritarian control. Yet, even within a debilitating zeitgeist, Orwell illustrates the ongoing nature of hope within society, demonstrated by the animals' idealistic visions of "green fields of England... untrodden by human feet." As such, the motif of hope is interwoven with Orwell's critique of totalitarianism to reveal how such regimes ultimately desecrate the ideals which constitute a sense of humanity.

CONCLUSION

Ultimately,[10] George Orwell's *Animal Farm* features protagonists who appeal to similar elements of the human condition; compassion, freedom and hope. In his novella, Orwell reveals the struggle for social change, whilst re-iterating these values which define humanity. Thus, a study of the text enables for a heightened understanding towards hope and what can happen when it is deprived.

8. This is a link back to the essay question.
9. Predeterminism is a philosophy that interprets all actions and events as being already decided by God or an external force of nature such as fate.
10. This is a minor point, but using strong concluding words like 'ultimately' and 'therefore' within your conclusion can contribute to the sense of finality and sophistication at the end of your essay, which is where your assessor will be deciding the mark, so making a good final impression is invaluable!

Essay Four

QUESTION: A text's context and form has a profound impact on the ideas presented. Discuss this idea with reference to George Orwell's novella *Animal Farm*.

ESSAY	COMMENTS
INTRODUCTION Dystopian texts draw upon contextual concerns to provide profound authorial perspectives towards harrowing political landscapes.[1] This is particularly evident within George Orwell's 1945 novella *Animal Farm,* which didactically portrays Orwell's subversive attitude to the despotic regimes of his context. In his literary portrayal of the Soviet Union, Orwell reveals the inevitable struggle for freedom and individualism caused by the insurmountable influence of authoritarian control. Yet, Orwell concurrently critiques the ignorance of his context, underscoring the role of the Russian society in remaining passive against the repressive policies of Stalin. In this way, the social and political context of Orwell plays a significant role in his construction of *Animal Farm*, as he allegorically conveys his contextual concerns towards the oppressive nature of the Soviet Union.[2]	1. Because this is an essay topic that explicitly calls on us to consider the context or genre of the text, mentioning points like this in our introduction helps to set the foundation for our discussion of specific textual examples. 2. You need to make sure you have a decent grasp of the historical context that Orwell alludes to just in case you get an essay prompt like this one! But in any discussion, knowledge like this can really elevate your analysis, so try to do lots of research regardless.

PARAGRAPH 1

Adhering to the conventions of the dystopian genre,[3] Orwell's *Animal Farm* highlights the impossibility of freedom within a political system that is propagated by the manipulation of the masses. This absolute control is reflected through Squealer's character, whose paradoxical capacity to "turn black into white" reveals a natural propensity to manipulate through the use of language. Likewise, Squealer's question, "have you any record of such a resolution?" undermines the reliability of human memory in recollecting the past by portraying written records as being synonymous with history. Thus, Orwell underscores the pervasive influence of oligarchical control upon the individual and the way in which it totally eclipses the possibility of individual thought, much like Stalin's cult of personality.[4] In stark contrast to the euphemistic "re-adjustment of rations" for the animals, the extravagance of Napoleon's "Crown Derby soup tureen" parallels the unjust prioritisation of state power over the wellbeing of the people, a vision that was shaped largely by the widespread famine incurred by Stalin's Five Year Plans.[5] The eventual restoration of Animal Farm to "Manor Farm... its correct and original name" symbolically highlights the regression of the animals' hopes and dreams caused by the pigs' manipulative tendencies.

3. Again, quick sentences like this help to establish context without needing to go into heaps of detail explaining a bunch of information that the assessor doesn't need to read. In general, it is safe to use words like 'dystopia' and assume that your marker will know what you're talking about. However, you have to make sure that you use the term appropriately and effectively.

4. This is a very strong explanatory sentence that links the evidence with the overall message of the novella, and then links this with the socio-cultural and historical context.

5. You should try to seamlessly include contextual links within your analysis of techniques and the text as a whole.

Drawing upon Orwell's contextual fears, this scene emerges as a compelling rejection of the authoritarian ideals which sought to impose complete societal control, revealing the deeply counterproductive nature of such values. Orwell extends upon this idea through the tragic denouement of the novella, as the chiasmus[6] "from pig to man, and from man to pig" foregrounds the pigs' seamless transition into oppressors of the farm. As such, Orwell's allegory of the Soviet Union provides complex socio-political discourse into the deeply manipulative and invasive nature of totalitarian regimes in their untempered quest for power.

PARAGRAPH 2

By extension,[7] Orwell utilises ignorance as a central point of characterisation within the animals in *Animal Farm* to reflect upon the folly of his context in allowing the manipulative practices of Stalin to occur. As an archetype of the apathetic Russian citizen, Benjamin's tendency to "understand, but... say nothing" highlights a willingness to exist in a state of passivity rather than engage with the corrupt activities of the farm. In addition, Boxer's repetition of his simplistic maxims, "I will work harder" reflect a crude mindset of perseverance and resilience, yet concurrently reveals an incapacity to think beyond the domain of labour. It resonates strongly with the psychology of Russia's working class,[8] who shared the fallacious belief that work would be the solution to their struggles. His high modality claim that Napoleon "must be right" further illustrates his lack of insight towards the scheming tactics of Napoleon in his endeavours for absolute power.

6. This is a literary device in which a phrase is repeated twice, but certain words of the phrase are swapped over in the second repetition. It is primarily used to draw more emphasis to a particular idea (e.g. 'all for one, and one for all').

7. Linking phrases like this are very useful in serving as a bridge between one discussion and the next, and ensuring that your body paragraphs don't seem like 2–3 completely separate and disjointed discussions.

8. For contextual analysis, it is important to show how the characters relate to the personalities of Orwell's context.

To a large extent, the animals' collective belief in Orwell's parody of heaven in "Sugarcandy Mountain" emerges as a naïve desire to seek hope and comfort within a realm beyond reality. In this way, Orwell satirises[9] the religious discourse of the Russian Orthodox Church, validating the Marxist perception of religion as being "the opium of the people." Despite the growing tensions between the animals' hopes and their reality, the persistent belief in "green fields of England... untrodden by human feet" expounds their sense of removal from the reality of the oppression that they are faced with. In this sense, this memory of Major's vision serves as a parable for the animals' desperate attempt to reclaim the freedom and individuality that has been totally eclipsed by social repression. Hence, Orwell's *Animal Farm* allegorically illustrates[10] and criticises the social attitudes prevalent in 20th century Russia which were responsible for perpetuating Stalin's quest for supremacy.

CONCLUSION

Overall, Orwell's *Animal Farm* explores the perverse enforcement of societal orthodoxy within a totalitarian society. Correlating with his views as a democratic socialist, Orwell satirises the ideological foundations of totalitarianism through the complete subversion of Major's ideals. However, by extension, he provides a distinct contextual perspective towards the ignorance of Russian populace in failing to act against Stalin. In this sense, it becomes a universally perennial truth that context plays a large role in shaping the ideas presented by a composer.

9. A good essay should focus on 'authorial intent' (i.e. why does the author write this, how do they show this, and to what end). I prefer to set this up as 'this is what the book is saying, and this is how the author achieves this.'

10. It's also vitally important to draw attention to the point you're making, rather than stopping at giving evidence. You need to show exactly what you mean – your essays should be mainly analysis, rather than a recap of the book.